THE COOPER STREET OFFENSE

A Philosophy for Reaching, Teaching and Discipling Black and Hispanic/Latino Students in Inner-City Schools

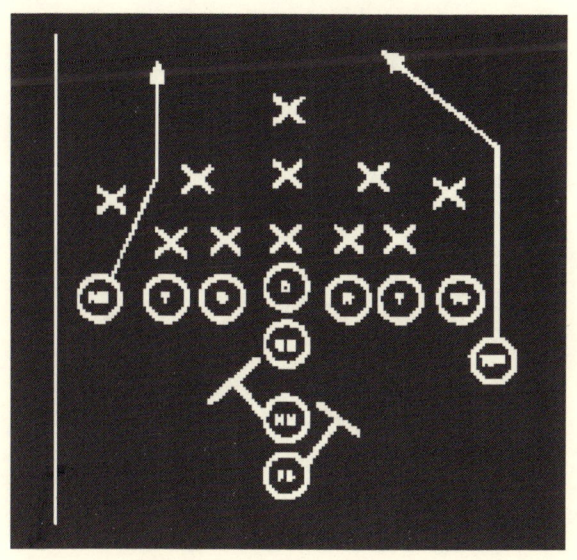

R. Rakeem Miller

CreateSpace Independent Publishing Platform
100 Enterprise Way, Suite A200
Scotts Valley, CA 95066

Copyright © 2013 by Randy R. Miller Sr.
All rights reserved. No part of this publication
may be reproduced or transmitted in any
form or by any means, electronic or mechanical,
including photocopy, recording, or any
information storage and retrieval systems,
without permission in writing from
the publisher.

Any additional questions about permissions can
be submitted by email to
rrmiller83@gmail.com

ISBN-13: 978-1482775716
ISBN-10: 1482775719

Manufactured in the United States

Cover Design: Amazon Create Space
Cover Picture: Randy R. Miller Sr.
Editorial Production: Manifesting Opportunities for Renewal and Empowerment, Inc.
Typography: Randy R. Miller Sr.

DEDICATION:

To The Students of the LEAP Academy University Charter School

Without the many lessons you have taught me, this document would not have been possible. I pray that I have given you more than you have given me, although I know that you've given me so much more.

THE COOPER STREET OFFENSE

A Philosophy for Reaching, Teaching and Discipling Black & Hispanic/Latino Students in Inner-City Schools

Table of Contents

Introduction

6

Chapter 1

Knowing Your Team

15

Chapter 2

Characteristics of Inner-City Learners

31

Chapter 3

Talk to Them Not Lecture Them

50

Chapter 4

Give Them Options

65

Chapter 5

Facilitate Their Hustle

76

Chapter 6

Judging the Case

91

Chapter 7

The Great Debate

100

Chapter 8

Using Technology Effectively

115

Chapter 9

Assessology

127

The Close

142

Giving Thanks

150

Appendices - The Playbook

153

INTRODUCTION

"The function of education is to teach one to think intensively and critically. Intelligence plus character – that is the goal of true education."

- Dr. Martin Luther King Jr.

I love sports.

In American society, sports have always been the great equalizer. In a country where discrimination, prejudice and fear have dominated the thoughts and motivations of many individuals throughout human history, athletic competitions have always presented people with the opportunity to prove themselves and display their abilities; an opportunity to overcome prejudices and preconceived ideas. Simply put, you cannot deny the skill and athletic ability of an individual no matter how hard you try; abilities and hard work always win out over the personal prejudices and/or personal preferences of individuals in a position of power, if not immediately then eventually. Unfortunately, other institutions in our society are not as cut and dry.

In any sport, there are a few key components that make up what many consider to be a "successful" athlete. Success in athletic competition defined as one who excels athletically in relation to his/her competitors. One of the components that successful athletes have is the "physical tools" that allow for their success — you have to have the hand-eye coordination, speed, stamina and physical mechanics necessary to play whatever game you are playing. Also, you've got to have the "intellectual tools" that enable success or the field or on the court. In order to play a particular sport, you must have the intellectual know how the sports IQ if you will, to think through various situations you may encounter while playing. Lastly, you've also got to have the emotional intelligence to play sports; you've got to have mental toughness to overcome adversity, outperform competitors who may be more physically gifted than yourself and you have to be able to push yourself to go above and beyond your physical capabilities. Take a look at all of those considered the great athletes in professional sports today and you will find all of these various attributes; Derek Jeter, Kobe Bryant, Aaron Rodgers, LeBron James and Sidney Crosby... all of these players share these attributes. Coaches help bring these qualities out in their players order to get the maximum out of them to achieve the desired goal of winning and winning a championship. The same is true for teachers and students; all students share similar qualities and teachers are the coaches who have the ability to bring these attributes to the surface to help students achieve academic excellence.

One of the hot topics for many in education circles is the racial achievement gap; that is the gap in academic progress when comparing students who are White with students who racial minorities, specifically African Americans and Hispanics/Latinos. Four main explanations for racial differences in achievement have been offered: genetic differences, differences in school quality, differences in family and neighborhood environments, even among children from comparably economically disadvantaged families, and student oppositional identity (Wiggan, 2007). Educators for the last 40 or so years have been seeking to answer the question, how do we bridge the achievement gap between white students and their Black and Hispanic/Latino counterparts – particularly in inner-city school districts? Year after year after year, new general managers and coaches are brought into professional sports teams to help turn a disaster into a dynasty. The same is true in our nation's schools – new administrators and teachers are brought into schools to change the culture and level of achievement. Like professional sports, some are matches made in heaven and others are matches made in hell.

In many cases, people say urban schools when they mean inner-city schools. To provide clarity, an urban area is a region surrounding a city and can refer to a city, town or suburb in some cases (National Geographic Education, 2013). To be more specific an urban place can be defined as a special concentration of people whose lives are organized around non agricultural activities (Weeks, 2010). When we use the phrase "urban" to describe the people in a specific location as it relates to schools, we're not accurately describing the group we seek to identify – children who are African Americans and Hispanics/Latinos who are considered to be of the economic underclass in American society. For the purposes of this text, I will use the term/phrase inner-city to describe the above mentioned group with respect to such students' geographic location of schools similar. The students I refer to in this text attend schools in the inner-city. These students attend schools in district systems that generally enroll high concentrations of individuals who are members of oppressed groups as well as new immigrants who may be victims of discrimination (Ogbu, 1995). Such inner-city schools are also characterized by their overall size, structure, levels of bureaucracy, administrative mismanagement, high teacher and administrative turnover, impersonal nature, and lack of funding management (Weiner, 2003). While the terms "urban" and "inner-city" maybe synonymous when describing such schools, educators and students, I will purposely refer to these participants as attendees of an inner-city school and/or inner-city school district.

When it comes to inner-city schools, teacher turnover is outright discouraging; continuity and consistency is often non-existent, thus the implementation of a worthwhile academic program never happens. Whoever comes in to an urban school or urban district, teacher or otherwise—specifically a school or district categorized as "failing"—they face unique challenges to addressing the "achievement gap" aside from the various external challenges relating to the impact that a student's environment has on his/her ability to perform; a system of discipline that is both inequitable and inadequate; content-wide curricula that is both rigid and irrelevant; school leadership crippled by the "politics" of education; educators more concerned with image rather than substance; a breakdown of school culture facilitated by administrators and teachers who are both ineffective and disengaged. For the novice teacher, or any teacher who cares for that matter, these challenges can be too difficult or overwhelming to overcome. In order to begin "addressing" the achievement gap, teachers, must be ready; being ready involves three things: (1) a teacher must know the composition of his/her team; (2) a teacher must have a game plan that the team can successfully execute; and (3) a teacher must embrace the reality that their classroom time with their students is the most precious time of their day.

What is meant by "knowing the composition of your team," is knowing the tendencies, the skill sets, the strengths and weaknesses of the individuals within your classroom. Having a game plan means that you have a few strategies and set "plays" in order to reach the goal of educating kids. That also means that teachers must also be able to adjust to what they see in the classroom. Lastly, teachers must be at peace with the realization that the forces that dictate which students they teach and the "standards" they must meet are beyond their control, thus they simply must do the job. Find me a successful teacher and I will show you a teacher who knows very well the students he or she teaches, one who has a game plan that the students can execute, and on who is successful in spite of the challenges posed to them by both their administration and policy makers. It is not easy to have a handle on any of these, but once you successfully tackle one objective, it will build your ability to tackle the others – each is a building block for the other.

In chapter 1, we start with the first building block: knowing your team. In order to reach any group of people, you must know the audience that you are speaking to. You have to speak their language, you must invoke their values and traditions in order to get them to go along with the information or concept that you are presenting. You've got to meet people where they are. When it comes to your students, they are not scholars just because you walked through the door. They are on the road of scholarly potential and your classroom is a highway along the path to leading them there. In chapter 2, we'll discuss the various characteristics that make up inner-city learners. We'll specifically be looking at characteristics that some people find difficult to deal with and exactly how and why these personality traits can be used to create productive and successful students and individuals. In chapter 3, we'll discuss the art of the lecture and how to make it more participatory in an effort to cut down the boredom of the students so they can gain the most in any lecture you provide. In chapter 4, we'll take a look at how providing choices in the classroom can create independence and ownership of student work by the students themselves.

In chapter 5, we'll be discussing entrepreneurship in education; student entrepreneurship specifically and how we can maximize on the capitalist desires of our students through project-based learning using our lesson content as an instructional foundation. In chapter 6, we'll discuss the use of case studies as a way to (1) reinforce writing, (2) better engage students in your lesson and (3) with completing homework. In chapter 7, we'll take a look at how debating can change the dynamic of your classroom and provide students with meaningful learning opportunities that go beyond the content. In chapter 8, we'll discuss the use of technology in the classroom; how your inner-city learners are people of technological advancement, how this impacts their ability to learn and process in information, and what you can do to create a better environment of learning. Lastly, we close out the book with chapter 9 about assessment: specifically exploring what culturally relevant and engaging assessment looks like in the classroom.

It is my hope that through this text, teachers can gain some strategies that will help them in the classroom. While many of these strategies and tips can be implemented in just about any classroom, these are things that are, in my opinion, very effective in the inner city and urban classrooms. If you recognize the culture of inner-city and urban communities, then you can create activities and curricula around that culture to benefit the student participants. In most cases, what separates those who experience frequent behavior problems from those who do not is their ability to keep their students focused on learning and intellectually engaged (Noguera, 2003). Coaches develop offenses and defenses most times according to the talent they have in the locker room. Teachers should do the same thing. When developing lesson plans and assignments, we must have the characteristics and culture of our students in mind. According to inner-city school statistics nationwide, the racial composition of the teacher population differs from that of the student population. If we (teachers) always make plans according to our experiences, culture and frame of reference, we've set our students up for failure, unless we (teachers and students) share similar experiences.

All of these strategies and tactics are things I learned while teaching in a school located on Cooper Street in Camden, NJ. While the philosophical framework isn't perfect, it has achieved some positive results for me and I've grown to become a better teacher. It is my prayer that after reading this book, it can achieve some positive results for you and make you better within the profession.

Chapter 1
Knowing Your Team

"Self knowledge comes from knowing other men."

- Johann Wolfgang Van Goethe

One of the most important components of being a good teacher is actually knowing the population that you are teaching; this means that you must KNOW your students – their environment, their culture, their history and how those things impact their behavior, confidence and mindset. Some might disagree and say that knowing your content or being a good classroom manager or teaching skills necessary to testing success are the most important aspects of teaching but they are partly correct. Knowledge regarding exactly who you are teaching is the primary building block for everything else a teacher does in the classroom; from teaching the content to managing the classroom. Many folks believe that children are all the same. There are behaviors and actions that all children take and equally there is a level of immaturity and inexperience that all children have. However, those things should never make a teacher assume children to be 1 dimensional. All children have different experiences, histories and attitudes which impact the students they will be in the classroom. Also, just because kids come from similar circumstances doesn't mean they are similar kids. You have to be a great discerner and manager of personalities... the same goes for how you deal with parents and administrators, but for the purposes of this book, I will focus on the students.

In many of our inner-city schools, teachers either lack or disregard the cultural awareness component to classroom management and instructional delivery. The racial makeup of the American teaching force is not representative of the racial composition of the student population in our nation schools. When you consider the numbers of Black males who are overly disciplined and undereducated, to not consider the racial composition of who teaches him would be a grave mistake. According to Howard University professor Dr. Ivory Toldson, of the over 6 million teachers in this country, nearly 80% are White (62% White female), 9.3% are African American (1.8% Black male), and 7.4% Hispanic/Latino (1.7% Hispanic/Latino male); there is 1 White female teacher for every 15 students and 1 Black male teacher for every 534 students (Toldson, 2012). If you consider the racial composition of inner-city school students when looking at the racial composition of teachers nationally, you can envision with relative certainty what inner-city schools look like, and it is indeed a problem that impacts every aspect of teaching and learning.

After prospective teachers leave education programs in the university setting for jobs in inner-city classrooms, they rate classroom management as one of the main challenges

(Weiner, 2003). Knowing the backgrounds of your students can help with managing and succeeding in any classroom, however it is not as simple as knowing the cultural traditions of African American and Hispanics/Latinos. Cultural competency for all teachers means recognizing and understanding the norms and tendencies of their student population(s) which are dictated mostly by societal, ethnic and socioeconomic influences. To be cultural competent also provides teachers with an awareness of white dominance and privilege in American society – that is the social arrangement of cultural and institutional dominance imposed on non-whites due to historical events and influences and how that dominance and privilege impacts societal interactions – and how it impacts the environment, learning and overall experiences of inner-city students.

We need to examine and articulate the values implicit in the western, white, middle-class orientation of U.S. schools, such as the emphasis on individual achievement, independence and efficiency (Weinstein, Curran, & Tomlinson-Clarke, 2003). We also must not be colorblind; while being culturally responsive is more than just race and ethnicity, we cannot deny the experiences and history of others in our attempt to treating folks equal by means of homogenizing and viewing groups as monolithic. While we ought to focus on improving student achievement, increasing proficiency in reading and mathematics, as well as encouraging our students to engage in the sciences, we must recognize that the structure and practices of schools can privilege select groups of students while marginalizing or segregating others (Weinstein, Curran, & Tomlinson-Clarke, 2003). Lastly, we must remember that the initial weapon of the school teacher is the relationship they forge with their students.

The common thread in all teacher-student relationships inside and out of the classroom is that they are relationships first. The job of a teacher is to be a mentor throughout the learning process. Unfortunately, the job of the inner-city school teacher is to focus on raising standardized test scores and close the achievement gap. Inner-city school districts need to get back to the basics; forging meaningful relationships between teachers and students and that starts with the cultural competency of teachers. When cultural diversity and race are not put on the table by the school but are perceived by students to be salient factors that influence their identity and school success, teachers who are culturally different from their students have a greater challenge in creating a trusting classroom environment (Weiner, 2003).

When it comes to sports, I am a huge football fan. Being from South Jersey would lead many to believe that I am a Philadelphia Eagles fan... Well, I am a closet Eagles fan. Before I say why, let me give a brief geography lesson for those of you unfamiliar with New Jersey. Our identity as a state is shaped largely by the psychology of being geographically situated between two metropolitan areas – New York City to the north and Philadelphia to the south – without having a metropolis of our own. Thus, if you travel to North Jersey, you can sense the NYC influences around you and when you travel to South Jersey you can feel the flavor of Philadelphia. Folks from North Jersey work and play in New York City and folks from South Jersey work and play in Philadelphia. In the summer, the entire state visits the Jersey shore; North Jerseyans have Seaside Heights, Point Pleasant, Belmar and Asbury Park while South Jerseyans have the Wildwoods, Cape May, Avalon and Atlantic City (North Jerseyans come to Atlantic City and claim it as a "state treasure" but it belongs to South Jersey). If you're from North Jersey, you grow up a Giants, Knicks, Jets, Mets, Nets, Yankees, Rangers or Devils fan. If you're from South Jersey, you grow up a 4 for 4 guy or gal: you are a Phillies, Flyers, Sixers and Eagles fan. If you grow up in either North or South and you like something that is a staple of the rival area, you're assumed to have a problem and in need of medication. Personally, whenever I am in North Jersey, I am ready to get back home to the south. When I am anywhere in North Jersey, I feel like I am in enemy territory. I am South Jerseyan; I don't like traveling further than Trenton and at the most, I'll go as far north as Rutgers University in New Brunswick or Six Flags in Jackson... I am and always will be exit 4 off the Turnpike; Camden/Philadelphia... but back to the Philadelphia Eagles.

Former coach Andy Reid was fired after a few lackluster seasons. Andy Reid was a good coach, but he never won the Super Bowl. He wasn't the most liked; not because he didn't win necessarily, but it's because his personality didn't always fit the area. Philadelphia is one of those places considered a "blue collar town." I am not sure how true that is these days, but when you consider who attends the games, many who fill the stands are folks who identify with the "blue collar" tenets of hard work and working long hours; underappreciated and undervalued by the "big wigs" in charge. When you look at ticket prices and the prices at the concession stand, it may cost a family of 4 over $1,000 to attend 1 Eagles game when you consider all the purchases involved. For some folks, $1,000 represents a paycheck or their rent. So if folks will be spending that kind of money on a game, they expect to be entertained and receive an outcome that will leave them satisfied, namely a win. When the team doesn't win, fans get angry and in Philadelphia/South Jersey, we don't just want to win; we want championships. When we are unhappy, we're gonna let you know about it. If you get tired of us criticizing you, just do your job, own up to your mistakes, improve as a player or coach and win games. Folks think of Philadelphia fans and think we're crazy... they think of snowballs at Santa or not appreciating great athletes. No, we aren't crazy. We want excellence and when you try to bull shit us, we call you on it.

For his sake, Chip Kelly better understand the psychology and the culture of Philadelphia. He better know his audience. Ownership has an obligation to please the fan base because the fan base buys tickets, purchases team apparel and pledges their allegiance to the team. In order to succeed here and make nice with the fans, you've got to "get" Philadelphia. In the same way the coach has to understand the Philadelphia/South Jersey environment to handle the pressures of the job, so too do teachers need to understand the culture and psychology of their student population in order to be successful in the classroom. Teaching is more than just knowing the content. Teaching is more than holding students to high standards. Teaching is more than thinking all students are capable of learning. Being a teacher does not mean you are a machine that processes through students each year. To be a teacher is to be human; it is to understand the human experience. Teaching doesn't happen by going through a textbook and having students complete a few worksheets. Teaching is meeting a student where he or she is, recognizing the variety of experiences that shapes their mindset, dreams and fears and having the ability to take their personality and improve upon it by showing them things they never knew. Teaching students is as much about challenging yourself as it is challenging the students you teach. The challenge for you as a teacher is recognizing that bland and basic instruction will get you nowhere with students, let alone inner-city students. In order to appeal to your audience, you must come to know them and intimately.

In my experiences, I have seen many of the daily conflicts between teachers and students. There is a disconnection between many students and teachers, and it hinders the teacher's ability to teach and the student's ability to learn. In part to blame is what Youngstown State professor Bram Hamovitch calls the conservative ideology of hope; that is inequality is mitigated by education, so if the individual works hard and applies him or herself in school, he or she will be appropriately be rewarded with social mobility (Hamovitch, 1997). The majority of teachers at the very least see, if not comprehend, many of the issues impacting the lives of their students and the inability of their families to be socially mobile, but many of these teachers believe that if students work hard and study hard, they will be rewarded with the opportunity for a better life and inclusion within the society they are not a part of. If that were true, I believe we'd see even greater opportunities for students of color. The reality is this ideology dismisses institutional barriers imposed upon individuals due to their ethnicity and/or class status. While teachers are well-meaning and they "care" about students and are "courteous" towards their students, for some, it is nothing more than a veil masking the lack of respect and appreciation of the background, values and traditions of the children and families that make up their school community. This in and of itself is discrimination; when teachers don't recognize that behavior is culturally influenced and when they devalue, censure and punish the behaviors of non-mainstream groups (Weinstein, Curran, & Tomlinson-Clarke, 2003).

It really doesn't matter how good a lesson a teacher has prepared or how smart the students in that classroom are. If that teacher has not done his/her due diligence with respect to connecting with their students on a culturally responsive level, students may disengage from the learning. When I speak of culture, I do not just mean race and ethnicity; one's race and ethnicity is an aspect of culture. Culture is defined as all the things that make up a people's entire way of life. That not only includes an individual's race and ethnicity, but also their religious beliefs, their socioeconomic and socio-historical background as well as their values with respect to issues of health & fitness, politics and other hot button topics. When you consider these things, although inner-city students may look the same, they are all indeed very different; the same can be said for the teachers. But when we compare student and teacher, we have a wide range of differences that can add a degree of difficulty in the classroom with respect to communication.

There are ways for teachers to help ensure that miscommunication is minimal in their classrooms. First, teachers should study the demographics of the community surrounding their school. Teachers should ask themselves the essential questions in order to gain an understanding of the student population and well as the community: who are my students, where do they come from, what do they value, what do they devalue, who is this community, what is the history of the community, what does this school mean to the community, what does the community value, what are the challenges of my students and the community, who do my students expect me to be, what do my students need me to be for them, what does the community expect of me in my role as teacher within the community, how do I gain the public trust? Educators must be careful not to generalize based on these answers or statistics they find while immersed in the researching of these answers. Your job is to gain an understanding. The answers to these questions are not black and white; they are complex and fluid. You should gain the knowledge of these facts to help you understand how you are to begin your task of educating your population of students. This information isn't always found on the internet or in community guides, but rather the information comes in conversation. Talk to your students, talk to their parents and to the community; essential knowledge is gained from hearing the experiences of students and families, particularly from the students, which are often disguised in the answers and opinions they give in classroom dialogue.

Second, teachers must step outside of their comfort zone and engage themselves with getting to know and understand who their students are by exposing themselves. Getting to know your students, on a very basic level, means learning the likes and dislikes of your students, learning the music do they listen to and finding out what is their definition of "leisurely activity" is. This is important, but as I said earlier, you want to know your students intimately. In order for that to happen, they must know yourself intimately as well. I am not advocating that you tell students your deepest and darkest secrets. What I am advocating is that you take the time to share experiences you've gone through as well as your likes and dislikes. The key is to show your students that there are many similarities that all people share within the human experience. When we recognize the differences between us as human beings, we can appreciate the similarities amongst us. Students often think of teachers as only mean and grumpy robots that bore them five days a week. When a student sees into the life of a teacher, outside of school, that student's perspective of that teacher can change. Giving a piece of the person that you are is more than telling students that you like certain types of music you like or if you are married. Giving of yourself means sharing some of your own dreams and fears; some of your triumphs and failures and what you've learned along the way. It's easy to provide basic information and move on, but giving more requires you to invest your time and emotion into the lives of other people. To do that can be draining and unfortunately, we're a society focused only on self. When we invest our time and emotions into our students and we allow them to do the same, going home each day after work won't be so easy. I don't suggest that you hold a group counseling session each day, but if there is a question posed to you concerning a collective experience in class, you should take that as a unique opportunity to make that particular day meaningful for those students. Teachers can take those shared experiences and information and craft lessons, projects, activities and even turn them into field trips. Using what students know and have experienced in combination with lessons according to your examples and experiences to teach your students what they don't know is a powerful method of making students comfortable with the content and concepts they might otherwise feel uncomfortable with. In other words, your students will trust you to teach them even the most difficult of concepts.

Lastly, teachers must allow themselves to be taught by their students to help them with instruction in addition to helping manage the classroom. To know your population is also to know yourself; to know your self is to know that you need to continuously grow professionally and that means growing in both formal and informal knowledge. Much of the informal knowledge comes from your students. Take classroom management for example. There are many books and journal articles that you can read to gain strategies on how to keep your classroom from reaching chaotic levels; the "magic" of this text is when the instructional suggestions do provide you with help with the management of your classroom. While formal knowledge is always helpful, in just allowing your classroom to simply "happen," you will witness firsthand the informal lessons on how to police your students. Often times your students will police each other. The specific aspects of culture; societal, ethnic and socioeconomic influences impact the expressions of acceptance, rebuke and discipline amongst the students. That happens both on the playground and in the classroom. You'll learn who the leaders are and their followers; you'll learn those who are quiet yet are independent thinkers; you'll learn who the class comedian is. With all of that information comes your opportunity to use it to make your classroom more efficient; informal knowledge in this instance can help you to not send your students to the principal's office for a disciplinary reason; and there is nothing worse in the eyes of an administrator than a teacher that constantly sends their students to the main office because that teacher cannot control his or her classroom. The knowledge that a student will not be penalized for their way they express themselves in a classroom changes the culture and environment of that classroom and can assign a level of credibility to a teacher he or she wouldn't have had otherwise – that is no excuse to not have rules in place, yet use discretion when handing out punishments. Contrary to what we may think sometimes, we (teachers) don't know it all. Learning from our students can help us not only teach our students but also mentor our students and help them when they encounter personal struggles, if necessary.

Becoming culturally responsive via knowing your population is one important way to close the achievement gap. Doing so can provide your students with the educational experience they deserve. Culturally competent teachers assure that the curriculum will be taught, that the curriculum will be delivered in a way that is responsive to the collective norms and experiences of the student population and that the relationship forged between teacher and student is built on respect and sincerity – a relationship where a teacher will assure that their students will not only learn the coursework, but grow as individuals. Here is what it will take: teachers who are ready to grow as individuals themselves. It was Malcolm X who said, "We cannot teach what we do not know and we cannot lead where we will not go" (Howard, 2006).

STRATEGIES TO IMPLEMENT:

- The prerequisites of being culturally competent are (1) recognizing that we are all cultural beings, with our own beliefs, biases, and assumptions about human behavior, (2) acknowledging the cultural, racial, ethnic, and class differences that exist among people and (3) understanding the ways that schools reflect and perpetuate discriminatory practices of the larger society (Weinstein, Curran, & Tomlinson-Clarke, 2003).

- Do your homework; research various sources of information about your students and the community where you work.
- Take the opportunity to invest time and emotion into your students by sharing your hopes, dreams and fears and learning of the same about your students.
- Bridge the gap of cultural differences by building on the similarities of the human experience.
- Take time to learn from your students; many times your students can teach you more than any textbook on education
- In all your efforts at knowing your students, remember to be sincere and respectful at all times.

Chapter 2
Characteristics of Inner-city Learners

"It is not enough to have good qualities; we should also have management of them."

- Francois de La Rochefoucauld

Whenever a coach or scout is looking for a player with a particular skill set to fit their team, they have various categories of players to choose from. If you are a basketball coach and you are looking for a tall guard who is quick, can handle the ball and can shoot a medium range jumper, then there are various categories of players that you can choose from; point guards, fast players, athletic players, and etcetera. You may not find everything that you are looking for when you are looking for a player to fit your system, but you take the best of what is out there and you teach; you mold and motivate as best as possible to get the most out of that particular player for the benefit of the entire team. The same is true for the classroom, or at least it should be. Unlike coaches and scouts however, we don't have "options" on who we teach unless you are teaching an AP or upper level course in high school, but I digress. In public school, you get who you get; there is no choosing students. For many teachers who work in inner-city schools, they may or may not wish they had the opportunity to pick and choose. Rather, we get who we get and we're expected to make the best of whatever situation we find ourselves in... and rightfully so. That is what we get paid for.

Some teachers will say that they don't get paid to be disrespected or they don't get paid to put up with outright defiance and backtalk from students; aggravation was not a part of the job description these teachers say. Well, here is a newsflash for those teachers who make those comments... aggravation is a part of the job; what job have you ever heard of where people didn't get aggravated? Everyone gets aggravated at work regardless of what industry it is. Teachers are no different. It is not because the students necessarily want to make your job more difficult... well, maybe some of them do. But we've got to manage the various personalities in our classrooms each day. Depending how well you accomplished the recommendations of chapter 1, the tendencies, behaviors and responses of your students may continually catch you off guard. You may assume that certain reactions are disrespectful and overtly out of line. They may be to some degree, but in order to understand where certain tendencies and behaviors come from, you've got to recognize the characteristics of your students. In the previous chapter, I discussed the need to research your students. Doing the research means that you've got to study your students... every student you teach. Do you think that is doing too much? Well, what do you tell your students when they've got homework or tests in every subject and they ask you for a break? You should be telling them to push themselves and to get organized so they can do the best possible job. You need to follow that same advice. Push yourself to know your students. Study them; what gets them excited, what gets them bored, what peaks their interests, who in the class can they not stand, who is their BFF, do they have affections for another student, how do they respond under pressure, are they a procrastinator... all of these things are vital to your lesson planning, instructional strategy and ability to think on the fly and improvise when necessary.

Many of the more empowering experiences that I've had in my life have come in college. For example, at the culmination of each course, the professor hands out evaluation sheets and they expect every student to fill them out. The professor walks out the room and we are to get to work. This gave me an opportunity to advocate for a professor I liked or criticize a professor that I believed was lackluster. I also used this time to provide recommendations that I believed could help with the course for the next set of students taking it. It didn't matter to me if those reading my evaluation took it seriously or dismissed me, if someone took the time to create it, I was going to take the time to speak my peace and make my feelings known. How else would faculty or administration know how to improve if I and other students didn't let them know? The student evaluation is a great tool to help you improve as a teacher and gain information on your students to see where their strengths and weaknesses lie, as well as your own according to their observations.

I decided to conduct a little research of my own. I am no skilled quantitative researcher or data analyst with data sets and all of that... I am just a social studies teacher, but I took it upon myself to reach out to my students and see how they viewed our school faculty as a whole – in addition to understanding the characteristics of our students, we must see how our kids see us. I gave surveys randomly to a little over 100 students from grades 9 to 12 in both high schools within my school district. Many of these students are students that I teach. I asked them a few questions about teacher motivation of students, parental motivation of students, and whether or not teachers care about the kids as students and individuals. After putting in all of the numbers, the results were astounding but not entirely surprising. The racial composition of the faculty within our 2 high schools during the 2012-2013 school year is as follows: of the 47 teachers in both high schools, 79% are White, 11% are Hispanic/Latino, 8% are other and 2% African American. The racial composition of our students is African American and Latino. I am the only African American teacher of record in either high school. In a school where about half of the students are African American, I am the only Black teacher they may come in contact with. In a school where over half of the students are Hispanic/Latino, there are only 5 teachers who are Hispanic/Latino and all of them teach, you guessed it, Spanish. Here is some of what I found out according to my research:

- When asked if students were always motivated or inspired to work hard in school by their teachers v. their parents, the students responded as follows:

	African American		Hispanic/Latino	
	Male	Female	Male	Female
Teachers	7%	16%	9%	11%
Parents	74%	73%	35%	79%

- When asked if students are rarely or never motivated or inspired to work hard in school by their teachers v. their parents, the students responded as follows:

	African American		Hispanic/Latino	
	Male	Female	Male	Female
Teachers	27%	21%	22%	19%
Parents	13%	2%	0%	5%

- When asked if students believed that their teachers cared about their success as students, the students responded as follows:

	African American		Hispanic/Latino	
	Male	Female	Male	Female
Yes	80%	47%	61%	62%
No	13%	9%	0%	11%

- When asked if students believed that their teachers cared about them as individuals, the students responded as follows:

	African Americans		Hispanic/Latino	
	Male	Female	Male	Female
Yes	46%	40%	30%	43%
No	27%	11%	0%	11%

When you consider how the students at my school feel about myself and my colleagues, the data here speaks for itself. I don't want to belabor the data, but there are a few things that stand out for me. Only 35% of the Hispanic/Latino males who responded saying their parents always inspired or motivated them to work hard in school versus 79% for Hispanic/Latino females. Of all the respondents of the survey, the highest percentage of people who were always motivated by teachers to work hard were Black females and that was only 16% of them; Black males being the least at 7%.

Of all the students who are either rarely or never motivated or inspired to work hard, 13% of Black males reported that their parents fit that description. Overall, the males are less encouraged to work hard in school on a continuous basis in comparison to females. This data says that we (the high school faculty within my district) are failing to motivate our students on a continuous basis and while some are getting it at home, all are not. Our male students need our encouragement and we're not doing the job. Occasional encouragement is not enough. We've got to constantly build up the self esteem of all our students. Society doesn't give a damn about the lives of poor Black and Hispanic/Latino kids. The next logical question for me is how do we (the high school faculty within my district) feel about our students? Do we think less of our students? That leads me into the next pieces of the data.

When you look at the students who believe their teachers care about them as students versus as individuals, all students responded that they believe their teachers care more about them as students than as individuals. Of course caring about our students as it relates to their success in school is good. Academic success can and does translate to success in life for many students. Also, the success of our students means that we care and that we are invested in their futures. While some do teach for those reasons, some teach in inner-cities because they couldn't find any other job period. I may sound cynical to some, but everyone doesn't teach for altruistic reasons. Nationwide, many students have weak and even antagonistic relationships with the adults that serve them, and report that they have very few teachers who they believe care about them (Metropolitan Life, 2001). Regardless of what we (the faculty at my school) believe about ourselves, our students say we don't care enough about them according to the data. Indeed, there is a drop off. Fewer of our students believe that we care about them as individuals and many are unsure. How can we reach them; how can we gain their trust and confidence if they don't believe that we care about the persons that they are? I wonder if we've actually taken the time to consider what makes our students tick. I wonder if we've taken the time to study our students in an effort to better tailor how we teach to them. I would encourage teachers to find out what their students think. The data may hurt upon first glance, but in the long run it will prove to be beneficial to teachers and students. Thankfully, within my district we have received professional development to help us tackle these very issues. However, there is much more work that needs to be done. The same can certainly be said for public schooling in the United States.

Unfortunately, there is no crystal ball or fairy godmother who can tell you or me how our students are exactly. We can try to figure out their opinions of us, and that can open the door to seeing our students in a different light, as well as seeing ourselves in a different light, but when we consider inner-city students, there are circumstances that we may not be prepared for having to account for when working with them. Nevertheless, their viewpoint, experiences and circumstances must be understood in order to understand the features and profile of your inner-city learners. While all students are indeed different, there are some basic characteristics that inner-city learners share. The following is a list of those traits. This list is not representative of all inner-city learners, however in this list you will see some of your students; the descriptions will help you identify others students as well. Inner-city learners are characteristically:

1. <u>H<i>ANDS-ON</i></u> – in every classroom, you find visual, auditory and kinesthetic learners; inner-city learners are often kinesthetic plus 1. Your students want to get dirty; if there is a project or assignment associated with your lesson, they want to get in the mix of whatever it is you are talking about – as long as your activity is engaging and relevant. They want to learn by doing because often times, this is how they learn outside of school. Many students learn this way but for many inner-city learners, due to the socioeconomics that influence their circumstances & viewpoint, much of what they see and hear prepare them to grow up

very fast. There may not be time for exploration and inquiry, only replication and refining. In the classroom, it is not that your students don't have the desire to sit and listen because they do. It is that they are engineered to get to work. Many of your students come from hard working families, some come from homes with economic hardships and some come from broken homes with generational issues. In any case, many of your students are use to growing up quick. That often requires them to have the "get to work" mentality. If you associate captivating work in the form of relevant and engaging assignments with your content, you will see a difference in your students. This is not to say that only inner-city learners are hands-on, but it is to say that for many inner-city students "getting their hands dirty" is one of the best ways to internalize information.

2. *QUICK-WITTED JOKESTERS* – your students are quick to tell a joke or outsmart the next guy in a verbal exchange. It's not that they are looking to be the class clown, but like most people, kids look to humor to take their mind where they don't want to be or distract themselves from their present circumstance or to defend themselves. Students can be funny for the sake of being funny, but there is usually an agenda behind making just about every opportunity a humorous one. I've found myself getting frustrated with students for

whom everything is a joke. Most times, these students are seeking to achieve a goal or mask an insecurity of theirs. What teachers have to understand is that you will be a target of a student's quick wit if their pride is in jeopardy. It's nothing against you, but the agenda of a kid always looking to secure the next laugh or secure their "reputation" takes precedent. Going joke for joke with a kid or thought for thought can be very dangerous for a teacher. It's like walking in a mine field. If you intend on walking that mind field with a kid, be careful; mines can go off just as long as neither you or your students are casualties.

3. *OPINIONATED* – The saying goes that opinions are like the opening of your backside, everyone has one and everyone thinks that only everyone else's stinks. Other than a senior citizen who votes, no one embodies this phrase more than a teenager. They have an opinion on everything, no matter how uninformed, no matter how ignorant it sounds, no matter who it offends, teenagers have opinions based on the nothingness they think is substantive. When a kid under the age of 12 talks, it can be even worse, because they often repeat directly what they've heard from home or on the street without the ability to repeat it accurately and so they sound even more ridiculous. Nevertheless, your students have opinions and sometimes, you've got to give them an outlet to express themselves, whether you do

current event assignments or if you have classroom discussions. Those are the moments when you, the teacher, can correct and redirect your students and help them work through their thoughts on any given subject. Sometimes, when a student speaks their mind, you learn a thing or two. It pays to listen... listening helps you teach and it helps you and your students learn.

4. <u>WANT TO BE HEARD</u> – this goes hand and hand with number 3. Some of your students have opinions and thoughts about everything and they come to school super talkative. That's usually because they may not have the freedom to speak, inquire and critically think within conversations at home. Let me be clear, it is not because Black and Hispanic/Latino parents are uneducated and are unable to hold a thought provoking conversation with their kids. It is because culturally, children never question adults and any form of disrespect, questioning their motives being one of them, is not tolerated. Freedom of speech is not the rule for most Black and Hispanic/Latino household. You do as you are told and if you run your mouth too much and "get grown," then there are consequences. In an educational setting, inquiry is welcomed and as educators we desire to assist students with finding their voice. Educators understand that there is a time and place but students who are always shut down

don't necessarily understand that. It's not that your more talkative students just want to talk for the sake of talking; it may be because they are seeking to express themselves because they genuinely do not always get the opportunity to do so.

5. <u>DESIRE STRUCTURE</u> – Every child desires order. Kids want to be structured; they love routine. Unfortunately, for some of your students nothing outside of school is routine for them, other than instability and the unusual. A child without structure is a child left to fend for themselves in the wilderness with foxes, wolves and hunters. One of the best things that you can do as a teacher is structure your classroom and your activities in a way that reinforces stability. Consistency is the key. When you are consistently consistent with your classroom management practices, your expectations and the way you teach, you tell a student that this is how things are – a fair and stable environment – and you can trust that it will stay this way yet be careful not to marginalize a student. When a kid has structure, he or she can flourish. Your students know that. They may resist it at first, but you must out will them; which you can and you will.

6. <u>DEFENSIVE</u> – In the "hood," you grow up with thick skin. People are raised to protect themselves at all times, whether it is physically, mentally or

emotionally. Criticism of any kind is a "diss" and to get dissed is to get attacked and when you are attacked, you fight back. Students will fight whatever or whoever it is that they feel is attacking their strength, pride or intelligence. Weakness of any kind is not tolerated amongst students and so when we witness fighting of any sort in inner-city schools, the students aren't savages or barbaric. Rather, students, like any other person in any place within society, are asserting themselves and defending themselves as to not portray weakness where they can be taken advantage of or dismissed by their peer group. Our schools have a lot of alpha males and alpha females running around and their desire is for everyone else to know they are not to be provoked or tested. Many times, these behaviors manifest themselves within schools because they are often established and encourage outside of school. Teachers can be and will be a casualty if a student's pride or will is challenged. Going back and forth with a kid is never productive, however, if you must "engage with a kid," particularly one of those alpha males or alpha females, always pull them aside and speak to them privately – it allows them the opportunity to save face to their peers and it gives you the opportunity to correct and attempt to put problems at rest.

7. <u>TAKE THINGS PERSONAL</u> – this is not to get confused with getting defensive. This is a cultural thing. Blacks

and Hispanics/Latinos can tend to take things very personal because we are very personable people; we're very emotional and we can tend to leave our hearts on our sleeves. So when things happen in school, things that seem very minor to you, students may not know how to take things or receive such things. When it comes to teacher criticism of student work, students sometime think that you don't like them; they assume you think they are stupid, lazy and a bad student. Make sure that your criticism of a student's work is constructive and that you always begin a criticism with a complement. Emphasize strengthens, introduce what needs to be corrected and follow up with another strength. Done that way, the only thing your students will take personal is that you like them. Remember that when you gain the trust of a student, they begin to see you on a personal level; someone they can come to and depend on. Keep that in mind as you work with them.

8. *CHIP ON THEIR SHOULDER* – your students have something to prove; to you, their families, their peers and themselves. It's deeper than proving they can get an A in your class or straight A's for a marking period. It's about proving that they will not be another statistic; that they will rise above whatever in their environment desires to pull them down. Your students want to be the success story they often hear about.

Every assignment, task and/or test is nothing more than a stop on their journey to success in their life. Your students do care about success and getting good grades, but it is because they ultimately understand that education is their key out of their environment; they are just unsure of how because we haven't explained how very well. Help your students to channel their desires to succeed; facilitate their growth by cultivating both their skill sets, their outlook on life and their views on the world around them. Teach why an education is important through relevance; teach them that missteps and mistakes are often times the greatest teacher. Teach them to take calculated risks in life and that the most important person that they are accountable to is the person they see in the mirror each day. Teach them that they are not defined by what society says; that their identity is not tied up in material things or in money. Teach them that they only need to prove to themselves what they already know – that they will one day be great.

9. <u>REACT FIRST AND THINK SECOND</u> – due to the points made in this list about your students, their defensive and opinionated nature and due to their desires to be heard and recognized, when situations arise, some of your students may "shoot from the hip." Many times, our students react before thinking and that is when they make mistakes, for example when a student

challenges a teacher without knowing the facts, that student reacted before thinking. When a student thinks before acting, they usually make the right decision and say the right things. But our students are conditioned to react; reacting often means yelling from the rooftops that they have been offended and they will do something about it. This is the classic case of a student getting in trouble due to some disciplinary reason. Always caution your students to think before any action or activity on their part. They won't always adhere to it, but if you repeat and model it, it will begin to sink in.

10. <u>AMBITIOUS</u> – lastly with regards to this list, but certainly not least, your students want to be great in life. They want to do great things and they actually want to make this world a better place. Like you and I, many of them want to help their families and start their own families. They want to be comfortable and live good and fulfilling lives. Your students have dreams... big dreams. They want to do big things and make a name for themselves somewhere in the world. The classroom is the beginning of their dreams coming true and in their eyes, you are one of the gatekeepers to either help them or hurt them as they seek to make those dreams real. You must be sure to never kill their spirits. Direct their passions to something constructive, help them reach their potential and

recognize their ambitions come from a specific desire to make themselves and their families proud; their ambitions also come from the inward desire to "make it" out of the hood and to not become a statistic.

Although many of your students have and display a number of these traits, I want to be careful not to over generalize. Nor am I unaware that suburban and rural students share similar characteristics, yet the various cultures they've grown up in dictate how these traits manifest themselves within those student differently than inner-city students. Some of these characteristics that I have described tend to be viewed negatively. It is easy for educators to point the finger at Black and Hispanic/Latino parents; their parenting habits and personal struggles, especially when it impacts the student. Too often, teachers assume that poor, uneducated parents simply do not care, or that parents who are learning English as a second language have nothing of value to offer (Weinstein, Curran, & Tomlinson-Clarke, 2003). Yet no one is ready to have a conversation about the public policies that have created the inner-cities of our country; where poverty, unemployment, crime and violence run rampant. Politicians are concerned with advocating for personal responsibility, but only when convenient. If the folks on Wall Street and major corporations were made to take "personal responsibility" for their actions and behaviors, I'd be okay with folks telling a single mother of three to be more responsible when it comes to her decision making. But I have a problem when the rich are allowed to get richer via deregulation of the financial sector and when corporations are allowed to advertise and market their physically, economically and psychologically unhealthy products to our youth but a single mother struggling to work and raise a child is told she should have been careful who she laid down with, and thus she must live with the consequences. When it comes to the bastardization and abandonment of our children, we are all to blame.

Your students may or may not exhibit most of these characteristics on any given day. Some days, we can deal with them, and other days, we pull our hair out. But we've at the very least must be able to identify them and understand where such behaviors and attitudes come from. If not, we'll be sinking rather than swimming. In the classroom, it's not about if you can do the breaststroke or the backstroke... it's about staying afloat. Having an understanding of student behavior can at least keep your head above water. Chapters 3 through 8 will help you get ready for the Olympics games held from September to June.

CHAPTER 3
TALK TO THEM NOT LECTURE THEM

"Some people talk in their sleep. Lecturers talk while other people sleep."

- Albert Camus

I remember sitting in a college class... it may have been comparative politics or Middle Eastern politics. Either way, I remember it being early in the morning, I around 9am or 10am. Our professor came as she did in each class; she'd sit at the desk at the front of the room, take out the textbook she required for the course, greet the class and proceed to read word for word out of the text, with room for occasional commentary – this was her idea of a class lecture. I believe this was a Tuesday/Thursday course, which meant that it was an hour twenty minute class; I had to sit through the reading of a textbook with an occasional mention of something that came from something other than the textbook. Now I never actually took the time or interest to watch paint dry, but I do believe that would have been a better use of my time than sitting listening to that professor. She may have been good with respect to her research area, but she was horrible at taking that knowledge and verbalizing it. Simply put, she was a bad teacher. I was not engaged in the slightest. It's a wonder I didn't cut every class.

I am sure that many individuals can think of experiences like that one. Unfortunately, many of us have had more classroom experiences like this than we wish to admit, particularly in high school. I am sure the memories get worse the further back you go. A large body of research on high schools shows that many students are bored, academically unengaged and deeply alienated in school (Newmann, 1992; Steinberg, 1996). High school was absolutely dreadful for me. Just about every class in my opinion was a waste of my time. There was no fun had in high school while in class. I can honestly think of only three classes that I actually enjoyed going to in 4 years of high school; that is a shame. I try to keep that in mind as I teach. Sure, as a teacher, it can get to be a bit nerve racking that you have to be entertaining and engaging when you teach, especially when administrators are holding you to deadlines and standardize testing guidelines. Either way, lectures are not supposed to happen the way they did for me in that college classroom. High school students should enjoy more than 3 classes throughout their entire high school experience. However, I wasn't the first to dislike the learning experience in high school and I doubt that I will be the very last.

Teachers can sometimes get excited about a topic that no one else cares about. That is good because the students cannot be taught by someone who is not excited about specified content. If you cannot get excited about the Declaration of Independence, the United States Constitution or the Emancipation Proclamation, then I don't want you teaching me – whether students get bored in your class or not students can sense authenticity; authenticity of knowledge and of care for them. The problem however is not persuading students that you are excited; the problem is persuading them to take interest in your excitement and to get excited themselves about the topic you are teaching about. Standing in front of the room isn't necessarily going to do it, although I think many teachers believe that it will. Standing up and "lecturing" to people on works best when you are someone they want to see with a message they want to hear. In many cases, you have to convince your audience to pay attention to what you have to say. As a teacher, you're an actor on the stage. But even before that, you are a salesman – you are selling a product and selling your ability to deliver it to the consumer. Your students are the consumers. Just because a person with money may have little alternative as to where they shop doesn't mean they have to make a purchase in your store. Likewise, just because your students have little option as to where to attend school, it doesn't mean that they have they have to listen to or learn from you.

One of the most transformative books of our time is *The New Jim Crow* by Michelle Alexander. If Ms. Alexander was coming to a local university to give a "lecture," I would attend; no questions asked. Once the lecture started, she would have my undivided attention (at least until she proved herself as not engaging and captivating). The difference between my students and I is that I would attend a 90 to 2 hour lecture on a 400 page book that discusses criminal justice, its relation to race/ethnicity and complex issues thereof that span 400 years – my students would not necessarily do that voluntarily. But if I was not happy with the lecture, I could get up and leave at anytime. If my students aren't happy with my teaching or "lecturing," other than taking a few minutes off with a trip to the bathroom, they have to sit through my lecture or they will suffer consequences to the decision of leaving my class without permission. The question comes back to the example of the salesman; what is the incentive to sell when you are getting paid whether you do or you don't? As a teacher, the hard work is done for you; your customer has been provided and essentially, you're getting paid regardless whether they buy what you are selling; in this case learn what you're teaching. This is why public schools can house bad teachers for long periods of time; it's because American society provides a free education, not necessarily a quality education. The terms "free" and "quality" mean two totally different things and each term comes with a different set of circumstances.

So then the million dollar question is how; how do you get students to give a damn about what you are teaching them while you lecture to them? First, you have to remember that as an adult, 1 word holds a different connotation than it does with a teenager. When you think of lecture, you possibly think about college; a professor standing in the front of a classroom or you think of a worthwhile lesson of some sort. For many teenagers, and you as well if you channel your inner teenager, a lecture is a negative experience where an adult authority figure, usually a parent, chastise you, corrects you and attempts to explain to you the error of your ways and how to get back on the right road. Teenagers hate being lectured to by adults, especially when it's coming from an adult who either does not care about the kid or doesn't care to practice what they preach. So when they sense a "lecture" coming on from you, the teacher, regardless of how great a lesson you intend on teaching, they become almost immediately turned off. So you never start off a lecture with a lecture. Start off any lecture with a question or a story that turns into a conversation that can set the tone for the entire lecture.

One of the worse feelings as a teacher is seeing heads down during one of your lectures; disengaged students who are not taking notes, asking questions and actively listening to your lesson. It has happened to me on a number of occasions. I felt like the worse teacher on earth because I know that even if 1 head was down on a desk, that I wasn't doing my job; the student has spoken with the head on the desk and as a teacher you have to adjust. If a head is down on a desk, ask if the student is sick. If so, send them to the nurse and if not, ask them to sit up and pay attention. Consequently, I've immediately shifted to asking a question or telling a story as it relates to the lesson – it breaks up the monotony of any lecture. One thing that you have to use to your advantage is the fact that your students are kids. Regardless if your students are kindergarteners or seniors in high school, they are kids and they all share two common characteristics; all students are opinionated and they love to be told stories.

People, in general, have an opinion on everything. The youth have opinions too, but often their opinions are dismissed or stifled because they are younger. Many adults stifle the opinions of children, especially at home. For many students, the classroom instinctively becomes the forum where they feel they can be both creative and reflective; where they can voice their opinion and have their ideas heard and accepted. When a student gives his or her opinion, they actually allow themselves the opportunity to reflect. As they are speaking, they are thinking and when you respond with more questioning you engage them in more reflection. While students can purposely or accidentally take you off course in any classroom discussion, it is your job to drive every discussion by making your questions detailed and focused; specified questioning – socially and culturally relevant questioning regarding the lesson/topic of discussion. When you involve questioning and reflecting in your "lecture," you immediately make your students a part of the lesson; students now have an active role in their learning. Educators often talk about the lack of ownership that many students have when it comes to their education; rarely do we provide students with meaningful opportunities to engage themselves in critical inquiry and reflection. When given chances to think critically, not only do students respond to questions with answers but they themselves pose questions to each other. That turns the teacher into a resource for validation, clarification and explanation.

Your questions must be relevant; meaning that you have the bridge the gap between the theory and the mechanics of your lesson and the world that surrounds your students. When I teach about the birth of Jim Crow segregation in the United States, I am absolutely excited about every piece of history that the topic encompasses; from Black Codes to the doctrine of separate but equal. I know that while my students should care about the birth of Jim Crow, some of them initially do not care and they may not see the relevance in the topic. But I do know what my kids do find relevant; music, fashion and sports. When I begin a lesson on the birth of Jim Crow during the mid to end of the Reconstruction Era, I start with a few questions:

- *Can you think of any institutional (i.e. school, restaurants, nightclubs) procedures and/or policies that are culturally biased?*
- *Are any of these procedures and/or policies valid or are they meant to simply discriminate against specific groups of people?*
- *Have you been a victim of a policy considered culturally or racially discriminatory?*

From these three questions, I can generate a twenty-minute conversation with my students. I get all kinds of answers that cite examples of the first question from no white-tees, hats, hoodies or boots are allowed in nightclubs to there being an actual dress code in the NBA for players; a league with a majority of its players being African American. However, you must be careful because such conversations can blossom into a period long discussion. Regardless of how much fun you and your students are having, you still have to get through the lesson; you must teach it and they must learn it. Yet relevant and insightful questioning can help begin and maintain the momentum of any lesson.

No matter how old your students think they act or how grown they think that they are, your students are still young and all young people enjoy similar things. One thing they all enjoy is being told a story. Telling stories in your classroom is a win-win. It's a win for the students because they get to hear something interesting about you or something and it is a win for you because you get to show students that you're actually a person like them who has experienced things and knows people who have experienced things. Telling stories introduces the real you to the students and they begin to feel comfortable with you simply because your allowed them to look into a window to see a piece of your life or the lives of your loved ones. When I say tell a story, I don't mean sound like your parents and grandparents who tell stories of yesteryear of how they walked to school in 3 feet of snow with no snowsuit. When I speak of storytelling, I am referring to an opportunity to tell students about an experience you've had relevant to a lesson or a topic of discussion in your classroom; they will absolutely enjoy what it is that you have to say and depending on how riveting the story is, they may never forget it.

Another aspect of storytelling is actually retelling the event of what it is that you are trying to teach. There is a little bit of history involved in every content area. This may sound biased because I am a history teacher, but if you teach a content area that is not social studies, recounting the history surrounding whatever theory you are discussing may help students both understand and remember exactly what it is you want them to know. It is easy to retell stories of historical events; I understand, but it can be done in other content areas. You may have to get imaginative, innovative and resourceful, but if you can teach the history behind the lesson, it can serve as a way to engage your students and if nothing else, you have a fresh batch of extra credit questions for your next test.

One of the perks about being a teacher is that sometimes, we get the opportunity to develop a new course and develop the curriculum for it. I was provided the opportunity to do just that by my school. I, and a colleague of mine, developed a course examining racial injustice in the United States justice system with respect to the drug war. Our text for the course is a book I mentioned before, *The New Jim Crow* by Michelle Alexander. In the text, the author provides the reader with court cases that serve as examples to the injustices people of color have and continue to face; some in particular cases surrounding what is called a pretext stop – a pretext stop is a traffic stop motivated by a desire to hunt for drugs in the absence of evidence of any illegal police activity. It just so happens that I had a story to add to the lesson. While on a trip to Tallahassee, Florida to attend a funeral, I was stopped by a South Carolina state trooper. I was driving a grey sedan with New Jersey license plates on interstate 95 wearing a du-rag and a thermal shirt... and oh yeah, I am a Black male. Long story short, I was let go... no warning, no citation, no nothing. The trooper basically told me he wanted to search me and my car because I looked like a drug dealer and because I was so far from home, he had reasonable suspicion—a particularized and objective basis for believing I was involved in criminal activity, supported by specific and articulable facts—to believe I was trafficking drugs from one state to another.

When I last told that story, you could literally hear a pin drop in class, it was so quiet. All eyes were on me as I told that story and the real reason was because by telling that story, the students got a chance to see "theory" be applied in real life. We live in a world where people don't believe everything they are told on face value alone; for most people you have to prove whatever it is that you are saying or asserting. Students are no different and in fact, they are a bit more demanding, particularly when so many of our students are used to broken promises and disappointments. They want to see the thing that you're preaching is important in action. It doesn't matter if you're teaching mathematics, science, history or English… students need to see how (1) the theory applies to real life situations and (2) how your lesson relates to them personally. You might say to yourself that to show both those things in every lesson may be a tough task… if nothing else it is a tedious task, but if it that is what it takes for your kids to understand slope intercept, the war of 1812 or acceleration, then storytelling and questioning is what you have to do.

In addition to questioning and storytelling, one of more important characteristics needed to be a successful "lecturer" is having the ability to think off the top of your head; having the ability to adapt a lesson. There may be days where the storytelling or the questioning tactic doesn't work. So what do you do then? One wildcard I always use when necessary is invoking the classroom diagram or student skit. This is always good for waking students up. A skit to demonstrate your lesson, or a specific aspect of your lesson, is a powerful way to re-energize both you and your classroom, involve your students in the lesson, help students internalize what you are seeking to teach them and take the attention off of the lecture and put it back on the lesson. When in my U.S. History class, I involved my students in a skit to assist with my teaching on the great awakening. Having grown up in the Black Church, I was able to recall the passion and excitement of the worship experience and I channeled my inner Baptist preacher and recreated the 1st great awakening. 7 minutes and tons of laughs later, those students knew what the 1st great awakening was.

At the end of the day, it's about having a conversation with your kids. Conversations are how we learn and how we grow as individuals. When we talk and specifically when we listen is how we gather new information and refine already acquired information. Teachers are so concerned with not getting caught up in anything other than "teaching the standards." Teachers are pressured by administrators, administrators are pressured by the district office, the district is pressured by the state Board of Education and the state is pressured by policymakers who are under pressure to get re-elected by the very people who send their children to learn under all that pressure. It doesn't work. That is just dictating... that's not teaching. Students are memorizing at best... that's not learning.

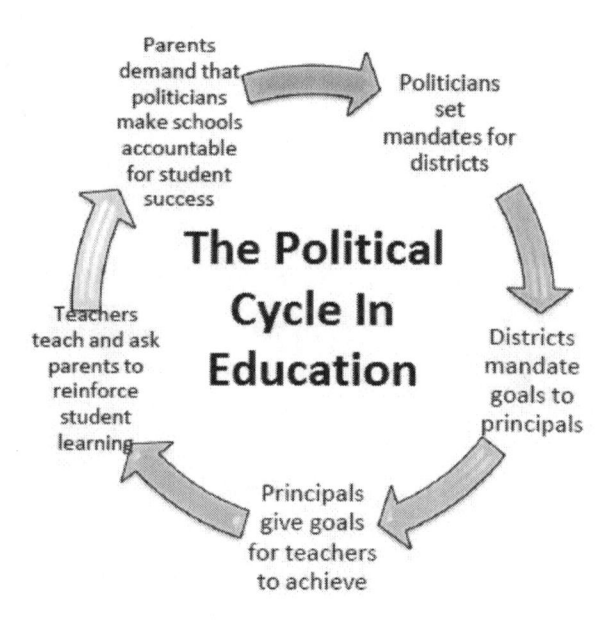

The Political Cycle In Education

- Parents demand that politicians make schools accountable for student success
- Politicians set mandates for districts
- Districts mandate goals to principals
- Principals give goals for teachers to achieve
- Teachers teach and ask parents to reinforce student learning

A teacher isn't someone who makes students copy notes from a board or powerpoint slides; a teacher isn't someone who dictates to students what to think, how to think and when to think. Someone that takes time to actually speak to you and explain a particular concept or idea, provide a visual demonstration either literally or imaginatively followed by a request for you to articulate or demonstration what they've instructed... that's what a teacher does. What happens in classrooms these days is a lot of paperwork, a lot of handing out worksheets, a lot of frustration and a lot of sleep (for students). And while a lecture is a style most suitable for talking, it may not be the most suitable for teaching inner-city high school students; and let me be clear, it is not because students of color have a poorer attention span in comparison to their suburban or rural counterparts. It primarily has to do with the environment and culture that shapes their point of view; everything is immediate, rapid, and the informal channels for getting things done have become the formal channels. Your lecture isn't going to cut it, not without engaging the students in the lecture/lesson. If you don't engage them, they'll sit there like I sat in that college class with my professor. You might as well be reading straight out of a textbook.

STRATEGIES TO IMPLEMENT:

- Never start off a lecture with lecturing. Start off any lecture with a question or a story that turns into a conversation that can set the tone for the entire lecture.
- Provide students with questions that are both specific to the exact lesson and relevant; socially and culturally.

- Your questions must bridge the gap between the theory and the mechanics of your lesson and how it relates to the world that surrounds your students.
- When telling a story to your class, speak on an experience relevant to a lesson, a topic of discussion or unit theme in your classroom – a story that is irrelevant is sure to put students to sleep.
- If the storytelling and/or questioning is not getting you the response you are looking for, switch things up with a skit or physical demonstration.
- If you teach a content area other than social studies, be creative and resourceful and research the history about the topic you are seeking to teach then integrate a small history lesson in your overall lesson.

Chapter 4
Give Them Options

"It's easy to make good decisions when there are no bad options."

- Robert Half

We can all think back to teachers that we absolutely loved, and of course we can easily bring back to our memory the teachers that absolutely drove us crazy. Now I've had some annoying teachers in my day, but there is only one that takes the cake… She was my 3rd grade teacher. I attended a small catholic grade school growing up. Up to that point I really didn't have many issues with my teachers. I had two teachers in Kindergarten and I enjoyed them both. I avoided a disastrous situation with the meanest of nuns in 1st grade when I was placed in the other 1st grade class. In 2nd grade, once again I avoided disaster. There were two 2nd grade teachers and one was senior citizen old and the other was very relatable for a number of reasons, primarily because she reminded me of my mom with respect to how she dealt with us kids. I didn't land in the class with the older teacher… I was pleased. But in 3rd grade, I was not so lucky. There was only one 3rd grade teacher and disaster could not be avoided. To protect the guilty, we'll just call her Mrs. O'Hara.

She was in her early to mid 30's at the time... she had a young son and was married. She actually became pregnant during that year. She was mean as hell. She had a smart mouth, she was condescending and she was always right. Now as a kid, I did talk a lot. I know I was probably a handful to deal with but she was always picking on me, or so my 8 year old self believed was the case. When 2 or more of us were talking, I was always the one she'd come after first. At the end of the year, I swore that I would tell her that I hated her. I got my chance on the last day of school when she pulled me outside the classroom to chastise me. I looked at her dead in the face and when she had stopped speaking to let me reply to a question, I just looked at her and I decided not to say it. Not because I was scared – I really did not like her. But I thought that saying something so mean as "I hate you" would have just hurt her feelings... specifically because I planned on saying it slow while gritting my teeth and staring her dead in her face, eye to eye while on my tip toes. I just said nothing and walked away.

At the start of 4th grade, she was no longer at the school and I was relieved. 4th and 5th grade had their struggles but I made it through. Then there was 6th grade and the dreaded monster of 3rd grade had returned to my school. I went to a K-8 school; grades K to 5 were in 1 class with 1 teacher while in grades 6 to 8 we switched classes. Mrs. O'Hara was the 7th grade homeroom teacher but she taught

Language Arts Literacy to all 3 grades. I couldn't avoid her. I was upset, terrified and in pain. I wanted nothing to do with her, but I had no choice. I remember walking into her class the first day; she stood at the front of the room with her evil smile. I sat at my desk—the desks were arranged in groups of four—and I watched her talk with that same condescending tone and all those memories of 3rd grade crept back into my pre-teen mind. Somewhere between the "pleasantries" and the first assignment of the year, Mrs. O'Hara began explaining her new system of doing all assignments for her class. Her new system involved something she called "optionals." What she meant by optionals was every assignment, whether it be classwork, homework or a project, specific assignments wasn't necessarily mandatory unless she otherwise said. We had a choice when it came to the assignments that we wanted to complete. She gave us a sheet with every assignment listed in a block format. Each time we completed an assignment on the sheet, we'd color in the block so that we knew we completed the assignment. For a 6th grader, it was a daunting task when you've never been introduced to a system of completing work on such an autonomous scale. I wasn't ready for that system; I was not responsible enough, there was no one to keep me accountable daily, and I was lazy. At the time, and for many years after that, I believed that the optional assignments idea was a little much for a 6th grade class. Looking back at it as a teacher, the system was innovative and actually, a good idea.

Hypothetically speaking, if you work at a school, say a charter school where there is an extended school year that is 40 weeks, optionals may not be such a bad idea. Optionals also are a good idea if your school has a minimum number of assignments that you must give. Whether you teach history, language arts, math, science... it doesn't matter; teachers can create assignments from assignments previously given. Teachers are like magicians when it comes to assignments; we can pull homework out of a hat. What I didn't see as a child I do see as an adult and as a teacher. You can imagine the hit to my ego when I had to admit that Mrs. O'Hara was actually ahead of her time with this system. What didn't help was that she left at the end of my 6th grade year and so she could not implement the system in the next school year, therefore giving myself and my peers a chance to improve our performance while in the system. If I had a chance to do it during 7th grade, I am sure that I would have improved, but we'll never know. Nevertheless, there were some students who flourished in this system, even students considered "disruptive." Giving kids "options" provides them with the opportunity to make decisions that are important with respect to their grade. One thing that we can all agree on is the fact that kids seek to be grown-ups. Many kids try to act grown and some kids in fact think that they are on the same level as an adult. While they are not, optionals can teach independence, responsibility, negotiation skills and prioritizing. If implemented, you will see a benefit to the students in your classroom.

I will use myself as a case example to show how optionals could work. At my school, all student work is categorized into four areas: (1) classwork, (2) homework, (3) projects and (4) quizzes/tests. All assignments must fit into one of those 4 categories. My students get assignments in each marking period according to the school's assignment policy. At the very least we must give: 20 homework assignments, 20 classwork assignments, 2 projects and 5 quizzes and/or tests. Our school year is 40 weeks long; each marking period is 10 weeks. Using the system of optional assignments maybe tedious and time consuming for you as a teacher because you are constantly ensuring that you have enough options for your students and because all of the grading you'll be doing, but the life skill lessons that you'll be providing through this process will be invaluable. Here is an example of what the system looks like; I'll be using history as the content area:

	Mon	Tues	Wed	Thurs	Fri
Week 1	HW - People & Places (Due)	HW - Case Study (Due)	CW - Writing Assignment	CW - Research Assignment 2	CW - Team Debating
			CW - Research Assignment 1	HW - Debate Outline (Due)	HW - Chapter Review (Due)
				Quiz 1 - Chapter 1 Only	

Week 2	HW - PEOPLE & PLACES (DUE)	HW - CASE STUDY (DUE)	CW - WRITING ASSIGNMENT	CW - RESEARCH ASSIGNMENT 2	CW - TEAM DEBATING
	PRO - BIOGRAPHY REPORT (DUE)		CW - RESEARCH ASSIGNMENT 1	HW - DEBATE OUTLINE (DUE)	HW - CHAPTER REVIEW QUESTIONS (DUE)
				QUIZ 2 - CHAPTERS 1 & 2	
Week 3	HW - PEOPLE & PLACES (DUE)	HW - CASE STUDY (DUE)	CW - WRITING ASSIGNMENT	CW - RESEARCH ASSIGNMENT 2	CW - TEAM DEBATING
			CW - RESEARCH ASSIGNMENT 1	HW - DEBATE OUTLINE (DUE)	HW - CHAPTER REVIEW (DUE)
				QUIZ 3 - CHAPTER 3 ONLY	
Week 4	HW - PEOPLE & PLACES (DUE)	HW - CASE STUDY (DUE)	CW - WRITING ASSIGNMENT	CW - RESEARCH ASSIGNMENT 2	CW - TEAM DEBATING
	PRO - BOOK REPORT (DUE)		CW - RESEARCH ASSIGNMENT 1	HW - DEBATE OUTLINE (DUE)	HW - CHAPTER REVIEW (DUE)
				QUIZ 4 - CHAPTERS 3 & 4	
Week 5	HW - CLASS NOTES ASSIGNMENT (DUE)	CW - UNIT I REVIEW ACTIVITY	HW - CURRENT EVENTS (DUE)	CW - RESEARCH ASSIGNMENT 1	CW - TEAM DEBATING
		HW - UNIT I REVIEW	TEST 1 - UNIT I	CW - RESEARCH ASSIGNMENT 2	
				HW - DEBATE OUTLINE (DUE)	

As you can see according to the example, there are a number of assignments to choose from. Since my school wants me to have students complete 20 homework and classwork assignments per marking period, according to the number of weeks per marking period (10), that amounts to 2 homework and classwork assignments per week. In my classes, we cover 1 unit worth of material in 5 week; I cover 2 units per marking period. Per unit, students are to hand in 10 homework assignments, 10 classwork assignments, 1 project and complete 1 test and 2 quizzes. According to the diagram, there are 20 homework assignments (4 to choose from per week), 20 classwork assignments (4 to choose from per week), 2 projects to choose 1 to complete by the end of any given unit and 4 quizzes; 1 per week and students must choose 2 to take. If a student doesn't take a quiz during week one and week 2, then he or she has made their choice to take quizzes in weeks 3 and 4. I would repeat this same format for every unit. Essentially, I have doubled the number of opportunities for grades for my students during the school year. That pleases administrators, parents and students (although they aren't even aware of it yet). This can work for any class and I would advise that this system be introduced in the 6th grade, just as Mrs. O'Hara chose to introduce it.

This system also provides you as the teacher discretion. You can mandate whatever assignment you wish to be a mandatory assignment. You can also make up rules as you go along. You can add or replace assignments as you wish. If you want to increase the number of required assignments, requiring 3 homework assignments per week instead of 2, you can do that. If you would like to require more homework assignments than classwork assignments or require students to take 3 quizzes a unit or that students complete 2 projects and choose from 3 of them, it is all up to you. In reality, the more opportunities for your students, the better; completing more work can help reinforce your lessons. You can also provide opportunities to improving grades within this system. It is a guarantee that some of your students will ask for extra credit during the marking period, especially if they are aware that their grade in your class isn't where it should be. If you notice that a class is not doing so well due to a test in the last unit, you can give extra credit for completing an extra homework or classwork assignment a week, for completing two projects or for completing 3 or all 4 quizzes during the marking period.

Creating optional assignments morphs your role as a teacher into a coach/facilitator. You become a general in the war room; you give the instructions and the plans and the student's job is to go execute the plans you've given. Mondays and Tuesdays are the days I would spend specifically for teaching; if I needed extra time, I would take half of a period on Wednesday and Thursday to finish or go over anything missed on Monday and Tuesday. Wednesdays and Thursdays are specifically for students to give them time to complete their classwork assignments during class time. While students are doing their work, you can provide time for going over lessons with students who need extra help—a sort of private session—and you can also schedule individual sessions/conferences with your students to go over any concerns you or your students may have. Of course, your students will have questions on various assignments and exactly what they are expected to do. This is a good opportunity to address those concerns in private, in addition to any discipline issues that you may or may not have to discuss. All things being perfect (although we know nothing is perfect in the classroom), if every student is working, you can grade papers, email your administrators and create new assignments.

These optionals also teach students the various costs associated with independence. Our students want to be treated as adults; here is their opportunity. They will learn quickly that there are consequences to all of their decisions, both positive and negative. As a teacher, I believe that learning facts and figures are good but more than that, I feel it to be most important that my students become great critical thinkers and great decision makers. Of course, no one is perfect; we all make mistakes. But if I can equip them in making better decisions by instilling in them a process for thinking and provide the experiences, positive and negative, they can refer to, then it is my obligation to prepare them. Many of our students don't take the time to appreciate that there are consequences to their decisions. With this system, they see a bunch of annoying assignments that they have to do; no matter how "fun" I make certain assignments, there is always the mundane chapter review and section review assignments. Nevertheless, they are getting an invaluable lesson on responsibility and how their efforts and decisions can and do impact their outcomes; in the classroom and in life. That was the lesson that I missed when I was in 6th grade. All I saw was the annoyances of the system Mrs. O'Hara was trying to introduce. If only I had learned this lesson when I was going through it, things may have fared better for me. Thankfully, I learned the lesson, so that I may teach it to my own students. Maybe, you should teach this very lesson to your own.

STRATEGIES TO IMPLEMENT:

- Provide your students with options with respect to the assignments they have to complete in your classroom; you can do the same with quizzes and tests.
- If you put in place a system with optional assignments, you should have all your assignments, tests, quizzes and projects completed for assigning prior to the start of each course unit; ideally, all of these should be completed prior to the start of the school year.
- Use the discretion given to you in this system to increase the number of mandatory assignments to be

turned in or to create extra credit opportunities for your students.
- While students are completing assignments in class, use the time available to either conference with students individually or host mini-lesson that review previously taught material.
- Implement this system in grades no earlier than 6th grade; introduce it to your student deliberately.

CHAPTER 5
FACILITATE THEIR HUSTLE

"So I start my mission, leave my residence thinkin how I can get some dead presidents."

- Eric B. & Rakim

I teach in Camden, New Jersey. The city has been known for being one of the most dangerous cities in the United States for the last decade or so. The population of the city is roughly 77,000 people. Here are a few statistics about the population of the city according to the U.S. Census:

- 38.4% of the residents live below the poverty level;
- Of individuals ages 18 and younger (24,452), 52.7% live below the poverty level;
- Of individuals 25 years (43,078) and older, 37.7% do not have a high school diploma and only 7.2% have a bachelor degree or better.

At the end of 2012, the city was approaching 70 murders during the year, a record. Competition amongst political and philanthropic stakeholders, the lack of real economic opportunities for residents as well as political rhetoric and political posturing dominate the apparatus of the city. The underground economy is one of the only things that thrive in Camden. With that comes conflict and with conflict comes violence, imprisonment and death. Also as the numbers indicated, there is poverty and with poverty comes a struggle for survival; crime, depression and hopelessness overtake the spirits of some of the people. This is the story told to people of Camden; a once bustling industrial center and now a devastated and forgotten concentration of violence, poverty and unfulfilled potential. That is the picture that many people see, but it is not the picture that I see.

I was born in Camden; I went to school in Camden, I grew up in Camden... Camden is my home. On these very streets did my friends and I rip and run. We played ball at the neighborhood courts then we refreshed ourselves with quarter hugs from the corner bodega. I've worked in the city... I work in the city now. My roots are here, my connections are here and my heart is here. I see the devastation; I see the corruption; I see the pain and the struggle of the people, but I also see the strength, the passion and the potential. I see triumph and I see defeat. I see the stories of both the told and untold. I see the presence of God; I also see unclean spirits. I see warfare taking place for the lives of the people, physical, financial and spiritual. Ask just about anyone from the City of Camden and they will tell you the same thing. Ask anyone from Camden about Camden and while they will make mention of the many issues Camden faces, they won't hesitate to profess their love their city; for better or for worse. When I look back to my youth and I see the potential I was filled with, I see the same in my students.

There are some other things that I see when I ride around the city... I see bodegas owned by individuals seeking their own piece of the American dream. I see hair salons that are full of women getting shampooed, receiving a fancy doo or getting micros. I see barbershops packed with fathers taking their kids to get a haircut or young guys looking for the tightest cut or shape-up. I see bakeries that supply many of the celebrations throughout the city with their cakes, pies and cookies. I see funeral homes that provide peace, comfort and encouragement for families dealing with a painful lost. I see hair supply stores, supermarkets, gas stations, dry cleaners, clothing stores, restaurants... These business aren't just located in the downtown area of the city, but they are also located in the less desirable areas of Camden; some of the most violent and "scary" areas are home to some of the more solid businesses of the city. If anyone is ever looking for me and I told someone I went to get breakfast, they can find me right in North Camden at Ruthie's. Whenever I need a phone case, charger or battery for my cell phone, I go right to one of the local stores that specialize in electronics. Whenever I am looking for a book to read or for a text to refer to when teaching, I go right to La Unique Bookstore around the corner from my school. If there is a parent teacher conference or some event that keeps me at the school later than normal, I take the quick trip to Parkside and order some platters from Corinne's Place for me and my wife for dinner.

Camden is full of entrepreneurs with wonderful establishments and without their services, the city would be at a tremendous loss. These businesses add to the flavor and culture of the city. In addition to that, they provide a wonderful example to our students. Our students are barraged with marketing designed to entice them to engage in consumerism: cars, jewelry, clothing, sex, and anything else you can think of. The key that unlocks their participation in the consumer culture is "money." The billboards, the music, the music videos, the television advertisements, and even within households; the message that our children hear is to get to get money by any means necessary. There are a number of different phrases and sayings that further promote this message but the message no less consistent. Left out of the message is that earning money the right way is never quick; it takes hard work and commitment to the task you've set forth. Our children are not getting enough of the right images. They receive too much of the pyramid schemes and get rich quick schemes that cost more than they can afford, expressed in various different outlets. As an education community, we have to make it our business to collaborate with community businesses to promote entrepreneurship; specifically promote the commitment it takes to succeed and hold as an example the various peoples who have succeeded who look like our students and come from similar backgrounds.

In addition to these examples, there is something else that I see; I see a different kind of entrepreneur that is demonized by consensus yet accepted by many within the community. The drug dealer also known as a pusher or hustler, although engaged in illegal activity, is no less of an entrepreneur than the person trying to get rich as part of public utilities or organic juice pyramid scheme. In fact, drug dealing is just like a pyramid scheme; one person at the top finds 3 people to sell his supply and he takes a cut of what they sell, letting them keep the rest. He continues to sell his supply himself as well. Those 3 people under him find 3 people under him to repeat the cycle. Now, I know I didn't just explain the cycle of how drug kingpins operate but the scheme is similar. Honestly, drug cartels function just like Fortune 500 companies; the kingpin is the CEO and his lieutenants function as his VP's. He has a product that he sells, he has factories where he manufactures his product and stores to distribute it. He has an extensive payroll list which includes factory workers, sales representatives, research and development, accountants and lawyers. Many of the young dealers, who are nowhere near the top, work essentially for themselves. They know the risk (whether or not they appreciate the risk is a different discussion) when they get involved, yet they see the reward – fast money; where else can you stand on a corner all day and bring home up to a stack, or even more in some cases (a stack is $1,000 in case you weren't sure)?

We, as an education community, don't like to think in any way other than negative when we speak of drug dealing because there is nothing positive about a drug dealer or the business of selling drugs... I don't believe that to be entirely true. When we think back to comic books and superheroes and evil villains, there really isn't much of a difference between the villain and the hero. Sure, they may have had different kinds of super powers, but both had super powers. The only difference between the two is that one used their power for evil and the other used their power for good. The same is true for the legitimate businessman and the drug dealer. The legitimate businessman uses his skills to not only make a profit, but serve people who want his services; ultimately providing a benefit to the community—notice I said the legitimate businessman; there are illegitimate businessmen who are out for self and bring as much, if not more, destruction to the community and society as the drug dealer does. The drug dealer takes his skills and talents and he provides a disservice to the community; although a segment of the population "benefits," the use of drugs is harmful to the user and community. Yet various skill sets, such as interpersonal skills, strategic planning, accounting, networking, administrative and managerial skills are transferrable from the legal to the illegal and vice versa. So then how did we lose all of those individuals to the streets? If drug dealers, particularly those who we see on television on the news; the ones with black and brown faces, if they are so smart and have so much ability, why are they not in executive board rooms?

We, educators, parents and community stakeholders, always put a negative spin on drug dealing in Camden and other places like it because for inner cities, drug dealers serve as an example to us... They are the example of children who unfortunately fell through the cracks. Some folks love to point the blame at everyone else but themselves for the poor decisions that young people make. While young people do have to be accountable for the decisions they make to a certain degree, we too, the adults, are equally if not more accountable for their poor decision making ability. Our young follow our example, they choose to either listen or disregard us according to our behavior. Each young person that chooses a life of drug dealing has been failed by the collective society in one way or another. Most folks would disagree with that statement. Some would argue that no one can be blamed for one person's poor decisions except the person who has made those poor decisions. I believe that we have not held ourselves to a high enough standard when it comes to the way we cultivate our youth. Our youth are inundated with messages to seek materialism and consumerism when seeking validation, acceptance, healing, and security. They are told that having money will solve their problems and that acquiring the "latest" is what provides them with their identity. We've failed to protect them from these messages. We've also been distracted by our own insecurities and selfish desires to satisfy our own "need" for self-fulfillment. Our children see us chase after money, people and material things for validation. We've been poor models for how we want our children to be; we are a "do as I say and not as I do" society — that is not good enough anymore. Our children see the hypocrisy we live on a daily basis and it is no wonder that they don't listen to us. It should be no surprise that we lose too many of them; losing one child to the streets is one too many. The drug dealers we see daily are the potential that we've lost as a result of not doing our part as educators, parents and community.

How do we prevent this from happening? We have to recognize that many of our students in the inner-city are "prove it to me" people; they have to see it to believe it. Many of us are like that as well, but many of the students in inner-cities have been let down by family, friends and educators alike; so much so they don't trust very easily and when a promise is made, before they get hopeful, they want results. Not only do inner-city students want results, but they want to participate in getting results of their own. Learning for them is not always an "active" experience when in school, however when inner-city students learn "on the streets," its hands on; there is no time for homework and for practicing. You have to learn immediately and more often than not you learn as you go. Learning the lessons of the neighborhood, the "code of the streets" is vital to your survival. A person's life depends on the lessons they learn and how well they learn them. We have to transmit this same message to our students in school; that their very lives depend on what they learn and how well they learn it in school. It starts by making your students active participants in your lesson. Making them an active participant means giving your students an assignment or task to participate in... and not just any assignment; give them a project.

The idea of project based learning is to provide a different method of instruction that involves student problem solving, decision making and reflection concerning a complex problem; the teacher is more of a facilitator than director in this framework of learning. One of the best ways of doing this is to provide students with the basic theory or logic of whatever concept you are trying to teach them and follow that with a model to replicate. When it comes to a project to provide for your students, you can create one that falls into one of three categories: (1) a community service project, (2) a private enterprise project or (3) an environmental project. A community service project promotes not only giving back to the community, but it also encourages student involvement within one's community and it provides you (the teacher) with the opportunity to engage with students and community stakeholders. Students also get an opportunity to learn about the various institutions within their community. Private enterprise projects give students a chance to actually channel their desires to make money, but you (the teacher) can steer and focus their motivation and attention properly. You can teach them practical lessons about integrity and ethics in business; lessons that you can still make a profit by not harming people or society. You can cultivate the various skills of your students in an effort to prepare them for the business world. Ultimately, you can provide your students with an opportunity to experiences the business world by creating their own business where they engage in the marketplace. Environmental projects provide students with an opportunity to address many of the injustices experienced by people who live in inner-cities and the surrounding areas. Whether you enact a marketing campaign to encourage adults to bring a mug with them to the coffee shop they frequent to reduce the number of paper products use or create a water filtration system within the school water fountains and distribute it to school, such projects are a fusion of all three categories and they teach students the importance of the environment and how society is impacted by the decisions we make regarding how we treat it. For a clear picture of how such a project based framework could be implemented, take a look at the following diagram:

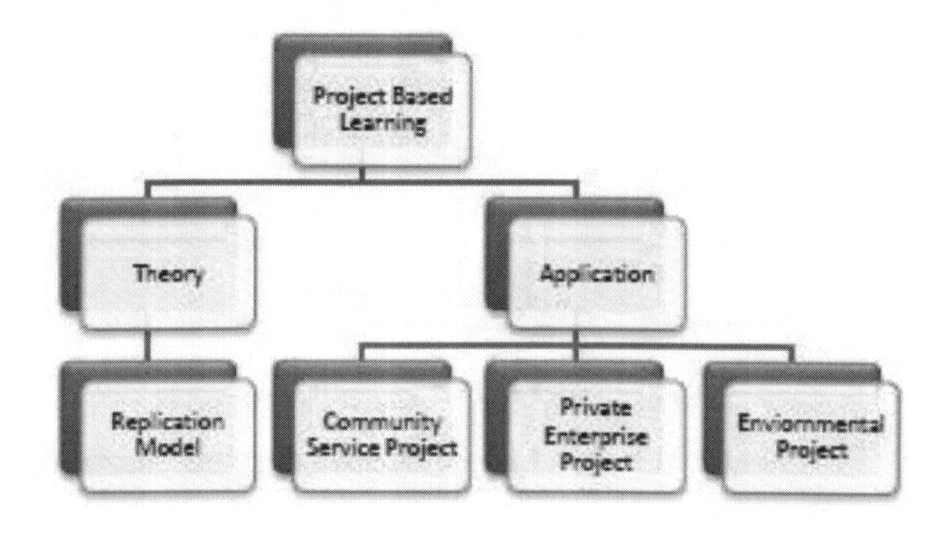

```
        Project Based
          Learning
         /        \
      Theory    Application
        |      /    |    \
  Replication Community Private    Environmental
    Model    Service  Enterprise    Project
             Project   Project
```

When following this model, make sure that you make the effort to take the needed time of teaching the theory and providing the modeled application of that theory. Remember, precision does not mean long-windedness. You can be very effective in your instruction without taking an entire class period to get you point across. If there are some students who don't "get it," and it may be some students, you can have other students begin the project as you take time to remodel the theory in action. Sometimes, teaching the theory doesn't work best. Modeling for replication by the students can sometimes be more effective. Once you model what you are looking for, give your students an opportunity to replicate your model themselves. Be sure that they understand that they are not to duplicate what you've done. Their job is to simply replicate the model and add their touch to it in the form of their completed project. This sort of framework can work in any classroom, with any content area and with any grade level. It may take more time and effort on your part, yet it is well worth all the energy you put in once you see student outputs. In life as in education, what you sow, you indeed shall reap. Here are two sample lessons of what your project may look like:

4ᵀᴴ GRADE MATH LESSON

LESSON TITLE	Athlete or Athlnot?
STUDENT LEARNING OBJECTIVE(S)	Students will strengthen their comprehension and skill with respect to fractions, decimals, percentages and division
RELATION TO CURRENT EVENTS	Sports and Career Options for Racial Minorities
COMMON CORE STANDARDS	4.NF, 4.NBT, 4.MD
THEORY & APPLICATION	4th Grade Math: Fractions, Decimals, Division, Rounding Numbers & Percentages
PROJECT BASED FORMAL ASSESSMENT	Students will create a report designed to compute the various averages of NBA, NFL and MLB players with respect to salaries and career expectancy to be compared with other occupations. Once assembled, students will create a report to be distributed to local high school coaches to be presented to student-athletes
INFORMAL ASSESSMENT (IF APPLICABLE)	Group Presentation of Findings
TECHNOLOGY & MEDIA USAGE	Findings Will Be Inserted in a Powerpoint Presentation To Be Presented To The Class and Others
INTERDISCIPLINARY CONNECTIONS	Language Arts Literacy: Public Speaking, Listening, Reporting
ACCOMMODATIONS	Implemented According when Specified

10th Grade Biology Lesson

LESSON TITLE	Welcome to the Shark Tank
STUDENT LEARNING OBJECTIVE(S)	Strengthen Students Understanding With Respect to Topics of Genetics, Energy, Cell Development and Ecology
RELATION TO CURRENT EVENTS	Television Show – Shark Tank (Entrepreneurship)
COMMON CORE STANDARDS	Various Mathematics & LAL Standards for Grade 10
THEORY & APPLICATION	Genetics, Ecology, Energy and Other Core Topics
PROJECT BASED FORMAL ASSESSMENT	Students Will Create Consulting Business Plans Designed To Address the Biological Concerns of People In An Effort To Make Them Healthier
INFORMAL ASSESSMENT (IF APPLICABLE)	Class Presentations and Proposals to Actual "Sharks" aka Local Business Moguls
TECHNOLOGY & MEDIA USAGE	Laptop Usage – Creation of Prezis
INTERDISCIPLINARY CONNECTIONS	Language Arts Literacy – Public Speaking, Presenting, Writing; Mathematics – Budgeting Using Percentages and Whole Numbers
ACCOMMODATIONS	Implemented According when Specified

Providing your students with the opportunity to be entrepreneurial through completing projects allow them a creative outlet to "get their hustle on." Your students are hustlers; translation – they are hard workers. They are willing to do everything they have to do to achieve their goals and what they want are the things that we all desire; financial security, a fulfilling career and a family that is provided for. Our students are willing to go the extra mile to make their dreams come true. However, they are often never given the proper picture of how to achieve their goals and the commitment it will take to get there. As a teacher, it is your job to provide them with perspective and give them an opportunity to exercise their abilities in a project that gives them experiences to encourage them. If they don't get those opportunities in the classroom, they will surely get those opportunities and experiences in the streets; in your classroom, mistakes will happen and it may cost a student a letter grade but in the streets, one mistake can cost students their lives.

STRATEGIES TO IMPLEMENT:

- Collaborate with community businesses to promote entrepreneurship projects and lesson within your classroom.
- Impress upon your students the positive examples of entrepreneurship and those who make money for themselves legitimately.
- Create projects that serve as a creative and vocational outlet for students desiring to exercise their entrepreneurial muscles.
- Prior to assigning a project, provide your students with a precise and targeted lesson on the theory of whatever concept you are trying to teach.

- When preparing to assign a project, you should take a moment to provide an example/model for students to replicate; students are to replicate your example, not duplicate it.
- As a guide, you can create projects that follow one of three specific categories: (1) a community service project, (2) a private enterprise project, or (3) an environmental project.

Chapter 6
Judging the Case

"We are all special cases."

- Albert Camus

One thing about the students that I teach is that they love to give a testimonial about an experience they've had and provide an antidote regarding how they dealt with said experience. Usually this happens when in the middle of a lecture, I make the connection between the lesson/topic of the day to a common experience we all share. For example, if I am teaching about pork barrel spending also known as earmarking, I would give an instance that is a common experience to explain exactly what earmarking is. I would refer the students to a time while shopping with a parent at the supermarket and once they reached the checkout line, as their parent was loading the conveyer belt with their groceries, you put a pack of gum in the middle of the belt as the cashier was checking the items to ensure that they would be "purchased" by your parent, because if you simply asked them, you may not have gotten the gum. I can guarantee you that at least 1 student would have a story to tell me about when they did that and what their parent did to prevent them from doing it again. These stories can get you side tracked and it can totally throw you off, but there is potential... not in the student telling their story, but rather the experience they've gained going through whatever it is they've explained. That experience counts for something.

Students have all kinds of experiences each and every day. When a random experience applies in the classroom and more specifically within the context of a lesson, you will find some students with their hands raised looking for the chance to tell their story. The danger is when a student has something to contribute to a conversation and you fail to let them; that can be the beginning of classroom management problems. One of the best ways to prevent this from happening is centering the focus to guard against off topic stories from your students. When you are teaching and hands fly in the air, you have no real idea what question or comment that student has. However, when you've set parameters according to the guidelines of an assignment or discussion, you are well aware of some of the major questions and comments your students will present as you call on them. Of course, creating an assignment is a way to get students involved in work, but that doesn't necessarily mean that you've involved them in an experience that allows them to use their experiences to help them address a situation.

For me, I try to accomplish that with an assignment in the form of a scenario affectionately referred to as a case study. I often give it for homework but I sometimes give it as an in-class assignment. A case study works great for a number of reasons. First, a case study provides me with the opportunity to provide my students with a scenario where they can provide their "expertise" and give their analysis and advise the class on how any given situation should be or should have been handled. We then discuss their thoughts the next day. Depending on the subject matter, discussions can last anywhere from 10 minutes to 25 minutes; I try to keep all discussions between 10 to 15 minutes... maybe 20 if the students are providing great insights. The wonderful thing about history is I really do not need to use a textbook. Honestly, I never use a textbook... for a number of reasons. I get most of my info from personal research via scholarly books or scholarly journal articles. That puts pressure on me as a teacher to create my own assignments. Creating these case studies can be a bit tedious; however I can tailor my assignments to my classes. I can use student's names and take a historical concept or event and I can make a more modern scenario and infuse that concept or event – making it relevant for the student. This makes giving homework a bit more pleasant because it has a little more purpose than reading and answering the section review of a chapter.

Also, case studies provide me with a legitimate opportunity to have students practice their writing in my class. My school, like all others, is very concerned with student success on the state test. The writing or constructed response as it is known on the state test, is a very important component to master according to my administration. I am not one to teach to the test however, I do believe that writing is important because writing is one way in which we express ourselves; it is critical thinking on paper. Our students need to be cultivated in that area. I make my students read their responses out loud in class. I do it so they can hear themselves how they sound on paper. Initially, my students didn't want to read aloud their responses because after hearing how unpolished some of their peers sounded in their writing, many of them reflected on their writing and became ashamed. I took time out to reassure them that they all sounded horrible. We got a good laugh, but I told them about how I was an unpolished writer in high school and how I got it corrected. Throughout the year, we continue to work on our writing through the case studies that I assigned. These are also a great way for me to connect with my English teacher colleagues and collaborate on assignments and back up their instruction within my own assignments.

What does a case study look like? Anyone can create their own case study. Depending on your audience, you can make it very complex or simplistic; you can make it expansive or limited in its text length. I usually make my case studies simplistic enough where my students can answer them yet complex enough where they need to think about how and what they will answer. I try to keep my case studies to a page; any longer and you may lose some students. People may disagree with this statement, but sometimes, you have to manipulate your students for the greater good for their learning. Some of them understand that whatever it is that you are making them do is for their benefit. Many won't understand and they won't care. When you have recognized the likes and dislikes of your students, you can create situations where you obtain more likes than dislikes in assignments and activities so that you can teach your content more effectively. A teacher is a maestro; he or she can create a masterpiece of an assignment on 1 sheet of paper. It may look like 1 sheet of paper, but the information on the sheet can be more than 1 sheet of paper's worth of work. Likewise a teacher can create a 10 page packet of work that takes less than 15 minutes to complete.

Below you will find an example case study. The particular example here was for my U.S. History II course. The particular lesson was on corporations, trusts, monopolies. The title of the case study is *Door Knobs*. Here is the structure of the case study followed by the actual part of the case study for this lesson as the example:

Background: Prior to the actual scenario, you must provide background information that sets up the scenario of the case study. Here is where you provide character roles, setting, theme and any other information needed according to what you are trying to accomplish.

Ex. *Raymond is the President and CEO of Richards and Sons Door Knob Company. He is in direct competition with Ortiz Knobs Inc. and Taylor's Knobs LLC. They each make door knobs and distribute them throughout the United States. They are the three biggest door knob companies in the country: Richards is ranked 1st, followed by Taylor's and Ortiz.*

Scenario: Here is where you take the lesson and concept that you've been teaching and create a situation that impacts the characters you've created; it is a modern dilemma based on contextual information.

Ex. *Ortiz knobs is the best at making metal knobs, however, Raymond was able to steal the chief metal knob designer from Ortiz Knobs by paying more $$. Because of this, Richards now makes better metal knobs than Ortiz. Now, Ortiz Knobs is about to go bankrupt. Richards and Sons aren't the best businessmen… they just steal and takeover. Ortiz Knobs knows how to administer their business. Richards approaches Ortiz with the proposition to pay all of Ortiz's debt in* *exchange for ownership of the company and Mr. Ortiz will be made a senior vice President. Taylor's Knobs speaks to Ortiz and tries to convince him not to sell to Ortiz and move forward with bankruptcy And rebuild his business brand.*

Decision: This is the point where you take the next step and create a question or a set of questions from the scenario; use the lesson and concept to create a problem based on the scenario that you created.

<u>Ex.</u> *If you are Ortiz's advisor, what would you advise him to do? Should he sell to Richards and allow him to take over the business or should he listen to Taylor? Is there anything else that he can do to help his situation?*

Activity: Here is where you provide the actual assignment. Of course, the assignment relates to the question(s) you posed in the decision portion of the case study. But just having the students complete the decision portion alone gives them no parameters to provide an answer. The activity gives structure to the decision portion of the case study. You can frame your assignment structure anyway you'd like. Personally, because I want to turn my students into good writers, I make them complete a 1 paragraph essay. I give them 1 paragraph because a paragraph contains all of the elements of a 5 paragraph essay and 1 paragraph can be completed faster than a 5 paragraph essay. I don't like giving homework so if I must (I must because my district mandates that teachers give homework), I want the assignment to be about quality, not quantity.

Ex.   *Write a 1 paragraph essay containing the following elements when answering the questions above:*

- *Introductory sentence*
- *Thesis*
- *Counter Argument*
- *3 Supporting Points*
- *Conclusion*

STRATEGIES TO IMPLEMENT:

- Create a case study when seeking to sharpen the writing, analysis and critical thinking skills of your students.

- When creating a case study, create a situation that merges the context and content of your lesson with a modern occurrence that is relevant to your students.
- Depending on your audience, you can make it very complex or simplistic; you can make it expansive or limited in its text length.
- Allow your students the opportunity to read aloud their responses as a springboard to classroom discussion as well as a starting point to improve student writing.
- When creating your case study, work with your teaching colleagues from different content areas; this allows you the opportunity to collaborate on this assignment. It not only helps your colleagues by reinforcing their content, but it helps you as a teacher with your content. Also, your administrators will look kindly on your cross-curricular efforts.

CHAPTER 7
THE GREAT DEBATE

"Debate is combat, but your words are weapons."

- Melvin B. Tolson (Denzel Washington)

One of the most fundamental things we take part in the human experience is talking. Talking isn't just something we do without thinking. As we speak, our minds are thinking about the next thought as the brain generates the words to articulate that thought to the receiver. One of the great pastimes as it relates to talking is arguing a point. Arguing a point is more than just talking; it involves thinking, reacting to what someone has said, internalizing concepts and understanding the rational for different points of view. One of the best ways to introduce to individuals how to properly argue a point is by debating. Debating is a formalized and structured way of arguing a point, with strict rules of conduct and sophisticated techniques to assert, argue, defend and/or refute a position. Debating is a great way to incorporate the teaching of various skills in addition to public speaking or the art of the argument. And your students, just like mine, are sometimes argumentative, often times confrontational and always opinionated... good starting points for making good debaters.

As a history teacher, it is important that my students are able to make the connection between the past and the present and specifically how the past can and does impact the future: both theirs and society's in general. As teachers of inner-city students, it is our duty and obligation to equip our students with the critical thinking skills and knowledge necessary for them to make informed decision as they progress through their lives. We cannot take for granted that they are getting these kinds of critical lessons at home. I believe that one of the best ways of doing that is by providing my students with a forum to discuss the issues of the day that impact both them and society. It is during this exchange of ideas and beliefs that individuals grow in knowledge and understanding of various viewpoints, stances and values with respect to a myriad of issues. Such development is vital to the maturation of individuals as critical thinkers, problem solvers and agents of change... if you give them the opportunity to speak, your students will indeed speak and without hesitation.

Formalized debate training will give students the skills to help them throughout high school and college. Students will need to be excellent researchers, excellent analyzers of text, excellent writers and good public speakers. Honestly, having these skills means the difference between student loans and scholarships; it can be the difference between having the skills to find a job and the skills to begin a career. In prepping your students for debating, whether in class or in a competition, you can ask your students to complete various assignments that involve reading comprehension, identity formation, and that require them to conduct research. You can have your students' debate against one another both as individual debaters and in groups as debate teams. These activities and assignments will cultivate the following skills within each student: (1) analytical approach to study, (2) critical thinking, (3) public speaking, (4) writing basics and (5) conducting topical research; all critical to an individual's academic, personal, and professional development.

I remember my first assignment as a teacher. I was told that I was going to teach a class on research and study skills. I was given nothing but a good luck salute. There was no curriculum; I eventually wrote the curriculum for the course. The positive in that situation was that I had the opportunity to build the curriculum from scratch, so I went to work. One of the things that I considered was creating a class that was both informative and interactive. It was a challenge. I taught 3 sections of the course to classes of 15, 26 and 43 students respectively… yes, 43 in one class. Quite naturally, each class had it challenges and I adapted where necessary with each class. I put together a system of topics to discuss with my kids: procrastination, time management, test prep and writing research assignments. My worksheets and lectures looked good on paper, but as I thought back to my high school classes, I quickly understood that all work and no play was no good. I had to integrate some play into the curriculum. I am not exactly sure where the idea for debating came from, but I got it and decided to incorporate it in class. While it wasn't perfect, my students responded to it. Like anything else, some gravitated more than others, but many took it seriously. Some of my students got down right competitive. I've had students cry as a results of their frustrations and the pressure involved with their performance. I've had students storm out of class due to their anger and disappointment with losing a debate. I've also had students gain confidence and learn that there is something that they are actually good at. I've had students who learned that it is okay to be intelligent and that it's okay to flex that muscle. I've also had students angry with me over how I've handled debates. Be forewarned... it gets intense.

In addition to all of those things, debating in my classes has given me the greatest joy of growing close to my students. I have had the opportunity to share with them lessons about life and society. Those lessons translate better than any lesson out of any textbook. During discussions about the economy, I've been able to discuss with them the pros and cons with choosing various careers as well as managing their needs versus their desires. During discussions about violence in the city of Camden, I've had the opportunity to teach about public administration and how poverty and "White flight" prevent tax dollars from being added to city budgets, thus contributing to the lack of resources available to a city like Camden. Conversations like these empower my students – they walk away from such conversations feeling more knowledgeable. We ought to reinforce to our students that they need to grow in knowledge. All of our children are born smart, but one must grow in knowledge to be properly prepared to meet the demands of this world. When we emphasize increasing in smarts rather than increasing in knowledge, we doom our children because they begin to believe that their lack of growth isn't due to their lack of obtaining knowledge but because they are not smart. If you believe that you are without knowledge, you don't necessarily believe that you are without the capability of gaining it, but if you believe that you are without smarts, then you could possibly think that you do not have the capability of gaining knowledge and we all know the famous saying: knowledge is power. Indeed it is.

Ever since that first year, I continue my debating activities and techniques in my other courses. I achieve many of the same results. The purpose for putting this chapter together was to offer some techniques and ideas to those who may like to try debating in their classroom and aren't exactly sure on how to go about doing so. This chapter will help you with integrating your lesson plans and curriculum with debating activities to motivate your students, get them excited about learning and to provide you with meaningful and relevant opportunities to teach your students about lessons that aren't necessarily contained in your textbooks. It is my goal to make self-assured, self-confident and self-defining individuals, equip to make decisions and defend them, with the ability to teach others how to do the same.

When we think of debating, we often think of the original tried and true method – two different points of view being argued with affirmatives, negatives and rebuttals. I use a form of this method of debating throughout my classes, with a pro and a con side. Often times, depending on the topic and question, my students may not appreciate the side they have to argue, but I constantly remind my students that it is not about what you are arguing but how well you argue it. This method of debating has its place and it is still relevant in both the classroom and in competitions. This is a great way to get individuals introduced to debating and it is a great way to prepare students to participate in formalized debate teams. But my ideas for a debating format is to stimulate thinking amongst my students to problem solve, challenge their values and belief systems. Not that the tradition way of debating fails to do that, but I like to infuse my own spin on the idea of debating to accomplish that goal better. One thing that I noticed in my classrooms was that the students had a high tolerance for arguing with one another, yet a low tolerance for organizing themselves when arguing. Some of the different ideas were designed to help them organize themselves better. By instituting some of these different aspects of argumentation, students stay on track and on focus. The following is the general structure for debating in my classes:

      PART I -   Opening Statements

      PART II -   Affirmatives & Rebuttals

      PART III -   Judge's Questions

      PART IV -   Open Forum Debate

      PART V -   Closing Statements

I divide each debate into 5 parts. Within my 5 part debate, I infuse different aspects of debating (questioning, argument, and presentation) into the entire format; I do this in an effort to familiarize students to the different components of debate. As I assumed when I started doing my debates this way, students responded better or worse to the different parts, but they all become familiar with each and over time, they worked well within the format. The first year I began teaching and I instituted debating, I used this same format just without the open forum. I added the open forum to spice things up a bit in my second year... that's exactly what it did. While each part seems self-explanatory, let me take the time to go into a bit more detail with respect to what I expect students do in each part of the debate.

1. <u>Opening Statement(s):</u> each side begins the debate by providing a short opening statement on their argument. It is the job of each side to tell the audience of voters exactly what they intend on arguing and proving during the debate.
2. <u>Affirmatives & Rebuttals:</u> during this portion of the debate, the pro side will offer their first affirmative argument. This is essentially their first major point to prove their argument. The con side will follow the first affirmative with their rebuttal where they will argue against the first affirmative posed by the con side. Each side will do this 2 more times with the second and third affirmatives and rebuttals.
3. <u>Judge's Questions:</u> here is the portion of the debate where I (although sometimes I will allow special guest judges and/or students pose questions) will ask each team a question in an attempt to delve deeper in their argument by attempting to poke holes in what it is they are trying to argue. There is always an answer to my questions, but the teams have think through the question they are given.
4. <u>Open Forum:</u> This is the part of the debate where I allow both teams to debate each other openly. I do not interrupt them, unless I need to get the discussion

back on track. Students go back and forth in a respectful and civil discussion on the issues. The debate discussion gets very spirited here. Also, if students did a poor job in their preparation, it shows here.

5. <u>Closing Statement(s):</u> At the end of each debate, the pro and con side provides the lasting impression on the voters to get their vote by disproving the opponent and promoting their respective arguments. What I usually look for is that each side tells the voting audience exactly what they said throughout the debate.

I am sure that you are wondering exactly what the non-debating students are doing while the individuals or teams are debating. The students not participating in the actual debate do participate in the day's debating activity. The remaining students are the voters for winner and loser. As the teacher, your job is to grade. You can create your own criteria for grading the debaters, but leave the voting to your class. I have a judges sheet for the students to complete that serves the dual role of an in class assignment that is an additional grade for me and as a scorecard for the student voters. Ultimately, it forces them to pay attention by having them participate as a major part of the debate process and my students take voting very seriously. Usually after each debate, I give my student voters an opportunity to offer questions and comments to the participants and the feedback the participants receive is often times excellent. The questions and comments portion after each debate turns into a peer review session; the questions and comments have less to do with the debate question/topic and more to do with how participants positioned their arguments, how participants left holes in their arguments and how the opposing sides failed to capitalize on miscues. It is a very powerful 5 to 10 minutes because my students are learning from each other; I consider myself a good teacher, but there are some messages that are more powerful as a student when they come from your peers.

So what do my students debate about? Since I teach history, there are number of ways I can go about creating topics. I could create topics according to where we are in the course of our lessons each week. While that would make more sense to do it that way as a history teacher, I go in a different direction. To keep the class current, I ask questions that deal with contemporary issues; my questions have to do with the topics of race, religion, homosexuality, the economy, criminal justice, education, sports and the environment. From these topics and more, I have over 100 questions that are given a bingo number and each time we debate, the topic question is chosen from the bingo ball. I could just as easily choose the question, but there is no fun in that for the students. The bingo ball gives them intrigue; playing on the Hunger Games mantra, "May the odds ever be in your favor," my students are in anticipation for the topic and question to be chosen.

From these topics, some very personal and provocative questions can come up as the subject of debate... and they do. Here is a 10 question sampling of questions that can be chosen at any time:

TOPIC	QUESTION
CRIMINAL JUSTICE	Should Ex-Felons be allowed to vote?
	Should Prostitution be legal in the United States?
	Should a minor (under the age of 18) who murders someone be tried as an adult?
	Is Affirmative Action necessary?
	Is the policy of Stop & Frisk a violation of the Civil Rights of racial minorities?
DISCRIMINATION	Does Racism exist in America?
	Should Blacks receive reparations from slavery?
	Are Muslims the worse treated than any religious people in the United States?
	Does an ethnic name hold you back from opportunities?
	Should English be the official language of the United States?

When it comes to the different content areas, you can structure your topics anyway you'd like. I would advise that if you decide to incorporate debating in your classes and you are a math, science, English, Spanish, physical education, art or music teacher, generate your topics according to both your lessons and the issues of your students' environment. Because your students live in an inner city, there is a wide range of issues that can be discussed; from failing public education systems to factories that produce hazardous toxins in the air.

You can also take these debate topics and questions to frame future assignments and projects. There is no specific way of constructing your format, questions and overall structure. You have the freedom to do everything anyway you'd like. However, I would ensure that relevance take priority in how you arrange the process within your course; if it is irrelevant for your students, your overall lesson of how to argue, how to see both sides of the argument and how to civilly disagree will also be irrelevant.

As you can see, some of these questions are indeed controversial and provocative. We all know that our students grow in homes where some of these issues are either discussed briefly, in detail or not at all. Our students come from homes where they learn many different things and they acquire many different views on various issues. Sometimes, our students acquire their views based on their own experiences; either due to their own struggles and challenges or based on the struggles and challenges of their peers. Either way, our students have their opinions about a lot of things. Of course, teachers are people too and we too have our views on a wide range of topic. Depending on the depth of our knowledge and experiences, our views tend to be complex. But it my belief that one of the major reasons why we are fractured as a society is because we are afraid to discuss our views in healthy and objective ways… the purpose of discussion isn't to convince others of how to think and what to think. The purpose of discussion rather is to expose others to different points of view to promote understanding of all sides of any given argument.

While I do understand that some discussions and debates are best left to the parents to conduct, our job is to facilitate growth. My job as a teacher isn't to teach a kid what to think about gay marriage, for example. My job is to teach a kid the various arguments for each side of the debate on gay marriage and from those points of view; the student will draw his or her own conclusions. But that cannot happen if I am not secure enough to discuss the topic in my own classroom. As I said in an earlier chapter, your students may or may not get an opportunity to explore the processes of their own thoughts at home via discussion and inquiry; the classroom is designed specifically for that. The classroom is the safe space for discussion and inquiry. Your classroom is quite possibly the only place where students can grow in this way; teachers have to be facilitators of this kind of learning. Your student will learn as you facilitate and teach. Remember, teachers are providers of information; our information can and will enlighten and change mindsets, but we are not promoters of beliefs per se. Debating does walk a fine line between conversation and heated argument, but as the teacher, you've got to drive the discussion; as long as you keep your students on task with respect to structure and procedure, the discussion will be civil, enlightening and also lesson on discourse, presentation and information. You may learn a thing or to yourself.

STRATEGIES TO IMPLEMENT:

- For many of your students, your debate activities are their first introduction to debating; infuse various formats of debate into your classroom format as best as possible to introduce them to the various forms of debate.
- Make your debate topics and questions relevant to your students; generate your topics according to your lessons, current events and the issues of your students' environment.
- Make non-debate participants part of the debate process by making them apart of the voting process and also by allowing them to ask questions and provide comments after the conclusion of each debate.
- Serve in the role of facilitator of knowledge and information; remain impartial, provide information on all sides of any argument and allow your students to reach their own conclusions.
- Place the emphasis on the processes and structure of debating rather than the argument itself. Your students will get frustrated about the sides they are given, but instill in them that what matters is how

they research, prepare, argue and reason through the argument; not so much the argument itself – It's not about what you are arguing but how well you argue it.

CHAPTER 8
USING TECHNOLOGY EFFECTIVELY

"Man has turned his back on silence. Day after day he invents machines and devices that increase noise and distract humanity from the essence of life, contemplation, meditation."

- Jean Arp

It is true when people say once you leave somewhere and you come back, there are things at the place you left that weren't there when you were. Sometimes, the new stuff is even better than the stuff that was there when you were there. I remember when I left my K-8 catholic grade school and I came back for the very first time to visit while in high school. The auditorium got a paint job, so did the hall way, offices got renovated, the library was expanded and the school got a brand new computer room with up to date computers. I said to my 8th grade teacher, "Where was all of this last year?" I got over it however. With respect to my high school, I'm not sure about all of what was new in the actual building, but I can tell you about the athletic parts of the campus. When I attended high school, the one thing I did was go to football and basketball games because we were pretty good and so was the competition. We use to watch football games in the stands on Saturday afternoons. When I left high school, the school got lights so now they only have Friday night home games... I was a little jealous about that one. In the gymnasium, when I went to the basketball games and I wanted to snack on something, I had to go in the hallway and there was a table where they sold pretzels and soda. I leave and the school builds a concession room with vending machines and a concession stand with choices of food, drinks and candy. I was a little mad about that one too.

But the one thing that left me the most jealous, angry and pissed off at the same time was how the creators of Microsoft Office changed up the software... a change for the better of course. When I was in college, I was a political science major and an Afro American studies minor so I did a lot of writing. With a lot of college writing there is a lot of citing. I had to input all of those sources... ALL of those sources – one by one. I remember when I finished my senior thesis; I had over 100 sources for the document. I had to manually type all of those sources into my paper and manually cite the ones I referenced in the paper with the help of the instructional guides. I get my 2nd professional job in 2007 and it is at a university. Of course they have all the latest in computer software. I was introduced to Microsoft Word 2007 and boy was I so sad to have this earlier. The greatest feature known to man offered by the good folks at Microsoft is the reference feature where you can simply input your source information in the specified areas and the software does the work for you. They'll organize your sources however you'd like: APA, MLA, Chicago... whatever your professor or publication requires, Word 2007 will do it for you. Before Word 2007, you had to take the MLA or APA guidebook and use it while you listed your sources. That was time consuming and a pain in the butt. Thankfully however, technology has made the difference ... Technology – the gift and the curse.

For me, Microsoft Word 2007 was a big deal. For our students, PlayStation 3, Netflix, YouTube, Twitter and Facebook are the big deal. Technology has made our lives both simple and complex. Our lives have been made simpler because of the mainstreaming of the computer throughout various aspects of life. I no longer have to go to a video store and rent videos like I use to do as a kid. Now, I can order movies on my local cable box. Before I started paying bills, I watched my father write checks and mail them out when he paid his bills. I pay my bills online the same day they are due. When I was in high school, I got worksheets and paperwork that I didn't want or need. In college, all of our assignments were given and submitted online; no paperwork involved. Technology has helped improve our lives in the areas of education, medicine and information. However, technology has been a detriment to our society as well. When I was a kid, there was only a 3 premium channels... HBO, Showtime and the only one my parents allowed me to watch, Prism. I could watch Prism because the movies on their rarely showed sex scenes. As a matter of fact, I only saw 1 sex scene on a movie on prism ever. Now, kids can watch whatever they want on YouTube or World Star Hip Hop without any parental guidance filtration devices. Facebook and Twitter have dominated many of our student's lives because the applications are so accessible via computer, laptop, Ipad, cell phone and e-readers. Students are both bullied at school and on social networking platforms as well. People can sell anything on services like Craigslist... game tickets, electronics and people as well. There was a "Craiglist Killer:" a man who killed people via finding his victims from Craiglist ads. Pedophiles can search for children and chat with them online and lure them to danger. Indeed, technology had made things a bit easier for the good to do good things and for the bad to do bad things.

When it comes to the classroom, technology can take either form: good or bad. As teachers, we often think of technology in a negative light. We tell students to put their cell phones away, we prefer to show videos sparingly and we often revert back to the "old standard;" overhead projectors and the chalk board... now replaced by the smart board projector and smart board and some schools don't have it or some teachers prefer not to use it. Some teachers just make powerpoint presentations... that is as technological as it is going to get with them, as well as with their students. Unfortunately, reverting back to the old ways or limiting technology is not good enough to get your student attention or get them engaged. Some would argue with me that you don't need technology to engage kids or to speak to their intellect or their interest. I understand that. But understand this; your students are children growing in the age of technology and innovation. Technology dominates their lives. If all of my friends gather for a house party and ask me to bring over some movies and I brought VHS tapes and a VCR, they would look at me like I am crazy and so would you if I were your friend and you invited me to your house to watch movies. So why should we expect to reach students without having an expansive working knowledge of technology? I am not saying that teachers should be like Steve Jobs or Bill Gates, but we have to be current and dare I say risk takers when it comes to integrating technology in the classroom. I don't mean just showing more movies from YouTube or having students use a smart board to answer questions. I am talking about making your classroom interactive and a technological playground.

Have you ever taken a drive through an inner-city neighborhood? If so, what have you observed? I'll tell you what I have observed in addition to the liquor stores, churches and restaurants... electronics stores. These stores may not be Best Buy or h.h.gregg, but these stores sell cell phones, car radio / car stereo equipment, televisions and computers. Just because there are students in inner-city schools who are economically disadvantaged doesn't mean that they are without such things as big screen flat TV's or the latest cell phone with fast downloading speeds. It is true that there are homes in inner-cities without the internet. Some of my students are without the internet in their homes. However, if your student has a cell phone, chances are they have internet capabilities on their phone. Most companies no longer make internet an option on specialty phones—phones that are marketed and advertised to young people—thus you have to pay for internet capability regardless if you want to use the internet on your phone or not. That point leads to your next problem; the marketing and advertising of technology to your students on an around the clock basis. Corporations understand that children don't have money, but their parents do. They also understand that children don't reason as adults do. Children don't think about budgets and priorities, they think about their popularity and their identity. Your students, from newborn to age 18, are inundated with messages designed to convince them that they need material things to be important and to be of value. This day in age, those marketed products usually involve technology of some sort.

I love reading books and so do some of my students. I have a Nook, but I love to go to the store and purchase a good hardcover book. However, my students may not share the same affection for an actual book. Maybe, they'd rather have a device where they can read books in addition to peruse the internet and listen to music. If I took it upon myself to be a sweetheart to my wife, I'd probably write her a poem; write it on paper with care and consideration with respect to my words and penmanship. My students know how to write, however if a young man wanted the affections of a young lady, doing things as I would may not be his first choice for wooing her. He may create a video or music or a montage using the internet or some sort of computer software so that he may profess his feelings. I have the luxury of being at the age where I am immersed in the world of technology yet I can go back to the way things were and be comfortable in either world. For our students, the way things are is the way they've always been. We've got to appreciate that in order to appreciate them and appreciate the ways in which we need to use technology to help bridge the achievement gap. I guarantee you, if you take a poor kid of color and a well to do White kid from the suburbs and you give each a cell phone with the same level of technology on each phone, no achievement gap will exist. So that begs the question, why is there an achievement gap amongst black and white in our nation's schools?

Plain and simple, within many school districts, the curriculum is slow, outdated, not culturally relevant and boring. Few students will be willing or disciplined enough to learn no matter how intelligent or mature they are... they may get an A but that only means that they learned how to get an A. Our kids live in a society that is fast pace and constantly in movement; should are classrooms be different? I am not saying that educators should abandon strategies that work, but I do believe that educators need to adapt and be courageous in their strategies to teach kids. We have to meet students where they are.

If reaching our students means that we have to speak their language which is the language of technology, then so be it. Here is how. First thing to do is to get some knowledge on the different technologies that your students are using on a regular basis; from devices to software to social networking platforms…familiarize yourself with them and brainstorm ways to integrate the technology in your lesson and unit plans. There are a number of great ways to use various devices and/or software for just about every content area and you can get as creative or innovative as you so desire. Next, you've got to find out what technology your students are most interested in. Sure, your kids have cell phones, but are they all into cell phones? Do the majority of your students use their cell phones for internet usage or do they have a tablet? Are they listening to music on an mp3 player or on their cell phone? Do they use their cell phone for everything or is it an option? Can your students make a video? Can they make music? Can they breakdown and rebuild machines and devices? You'd be surprised the information you'd find out if you took the time to do the research. After you do these things, get with the other researchers in your building, specifically the folks who work with your students on a regular basis – the teachers, counselors and administrators who know your kids as well as you do and compare notes. Lastly, you build your program: your lessons, assignments, projects and whatever else via incorporating your research on the technology and your students use of it. Here are some good ways to get students involved in learning with the help of technology:

	STUDENT ENGAGEMENT
Individual and Group Presentations (*Projects*)	Video/Film/Audio (Directing, Acting & Editing)
	Powerpoint or Prezis (Public Speaking—Art of Arguing & Persuasion)
Research (*Assignments*)	Lesson theme(s) correlated with a modern day problem/situation requiring online research
Lectures (*Lessons*)	Integrate videos, audio, current documents, quoted material from twitter

Of course in a perfect world, schools would give teachers whatever they asked. I want all of my kids to have an electronic reading device, but due to the budget, that is a wish to remain on the wish list. However, teachers have the awesome ability to be resourceful in the face of a flat out decline of their request or a dismissive disregard for their request. But even if we had everything we wanted, there is a variable that may or may not cooperate with us... the children. But here are some ways where we teachers can engage with the technology to help us to stay ahead of our clientele (who at times serves as our adversary):

TEACHER ENGAGEMENT	
Offer Online Lessons to Parents & Students	For absent students and parents looking for homework instruction
Information / Knowledge Sharing	For teachers looking to obtain from and/or provide strategies for teachers to improve practice
Networking	For job opportunities, professional development opportunities, and funding opportunities

Here is a sample lesson where you can integrate the knowledge of current technology and what exactly your students are doing with technology on a regular basis to help you to get them to internalize what you've been teaching them:

8TH GRADE U.S. HISTORY LESSON

LESSON TITLE	Celebrity Survey
STUDENT LEARNING OBJECTIVE(S)	Strengthen Students Understanding With Respect to the History of Civil Rights in America
RELATION TO CURRENT EVENTS	Social Networking – Twitter; Popular Culture Celebrities
COMMON CORE STANDARDS	Various Language Arts Literacy Standards for Grade 8

Theory & Application	Civil Rights Movement
Project Based Formal Assessment	Students will contact celebrities on twitter and ask them who they believe the most influential person of the civil rights movement is and why
Informal Assessment (if applicable)	Class Presentations and submission of a 1 page paper detailing the summary of their conversation(s)
Technology & Media Usage	Laptop Usage – Creation of Powerpoint or Prezi
Interdisciplinary Connections	Language Arts Literacy – Public Speaking, Presenting, Writing
Accommodations	Implemented According when Specified

At the end of the day, the use of technology is not just to use it because it is there. The use of technology must have a purpose. Without purpose, computer software and devices are as pointless as the standard tools of the classroom. Our goal is to both engage students in learning and show them that technology isn't just for entertainment and communication, but that it is also for learning and intellectual growth. The only way to do that is by modeling it to our students and providing them with opportunities to use the technology for that very purpose. Misusing technology will push your students away. Our students have been pushed away from us long enough – they've been pushed from our loving hands to the grubby hands of corporate executives who see dollar signs. We must get on the attack and take back the minds and spirits of our children. It starts when we use the weapons of our warfare in our favor rather than sit back and allow them to be used against us. It's time to get dirty, because the fight for the future of our students is no longer a fair one.

STRATEGIES TO IMPLEMENT:

- Research the different technologies that your students are using on a regular basis; from devices to software to social networking platforms.
- Research what technology your students use out of necessity and out of interest; there is a difference.
- Brainstorm ways to integrate the technology most frequently used by your students in your lesson and unit plans.
- Compare notes with other teachers, administrators and counselors on the technological interests of your students to gain a holistic picture of your student as it relates to technological consumption
- Take all of your researched information and build your lessons and assessments. Use the templates in this chapter as a guide.

CHAPTER 9
ASSESSOLOGY

"Knowing this, that the trying of your faith worketh patience."

- James 1:3

When it comes to my days in the classroom as a student, some of my worse situations involved when a teacher is going over homework or some assignment and I was called on unprepared; either because I wasn't paying attention or because I did not complete the assignment. The worst of all of these experiences took place in law school. The anxiety attacks were some of the worse I've ever had. In fact, I had no clue what an anxiety attack was until law school. I may have experienced them prior to my entry into law school but when in the legal classroom, those attacks hit like a Mack truck. Those attacks didn't come in all of my classes. I actually enjoyed my legal writing class, torts, contracts and even property. But it was that God forsaken civil procedure class. When I was younger, I feared the wrath of my parents... that class and my professor made my parents seem refreshingly understanding. My professor was relentless and I was struggling to keep up with the material. My other courses made sense, civil procedure however was as mindboggling as it was finding Osama bin Laden.

When I was a child, I displayed some features and characteristics in my personality that led many people to think that I would become a lawyer. Add what I like to call the "Cosby Syndrome" amongst Black households – the idea that many had that in order to be successful, you must either be a doctor or a lawyer like the Huxtables – it was a no brainer on exactly what I would be doing as a professional. Unfortunately, as I grew and matured, there was no one who developed or cultivated what talents and abilities I actually had. I loved to talk and I loved to give speeches and so people assumed that I would be a lawyer; teaching as a career never hit anyone's mind, but here I am. I enjoyed writing stories as a kid, but people assumed that was just what little kids did; write stories. No one ever presented me with the idea of becoming a writer and writing is something that is a passion of mine. So, with no one really looking for those talents and skills, I wandered aimlessly on the path to law, only to reach law school and realize that I made a mistake. I enjoyed law and I enjoyed learning about the law, but it was during the end of my first year, long after civil procedure, that I realized law school wasn't for me. Nevertheless, the experiences that I had while there taught me so much about myself as well as planted the seed for things to come.

My civil procedure professor, let's call him Dr. Lore, was an interesting guy; not because he was actually interesting but because he was indeed a character. He drove a beat up white Saturn and he looked too big for the car, like Shaquille O'Neal does in those Buick Lacrosse commercials; I never knew how he got out the car. He wore these funny looking glasses and he had the most insincere and condescending smile, but he was actually a very nice guy. When he opened his mouth, he sounded like a blue blood crossed with the speed of a slow talking old lady. He knew his stuff, but he was a horrible teacher of the content, in my humble opinion.. He would pierce his eyes through you immediately after he asked you a question and God help you if you didn't know the answer; it would become the longest period of silence in your life. Dr. Lore would stare at you and wait patiently until you found the answer he was looking for. Like all classes, this class was 2 hours... it was pure pain and torture, but I learned a few things while in that class; things that had nothing to do with civil procedure. I mastered the art of looking like I am reading when I am actually pretending, so I am not called on – I could have used that skill in grade school. I also learned how to properly execute the Socratic Method with a class full of students, as Dr. Lore so masterfully did each day we had class. For teaching me that, and about the process of discovery, Dr. Lore, I thank you.

One of the important things a teacher will do is assess the learning that has taken place in their classes among their students. The word *assessment* means different things to different people. To me, when I think of assessment, I think about measuring what my students know or have learned regarding any given lesson, chapter or unit versus the information they did not retain. From there, I can take that data to plot out my next moves; what needs to be reviewed, what I need to go back and focus on and what information I can build upon for the next lesson, chapter or unit. Typically in schools, we think of quizzes, worksheets, and tests/exams as the means to assess knowledge; at times, schools assess aptitude. Quizzes and tests are good indicators of what a student may know, but they don't necessarily help students internalize information; they help students memorize information more than anything else. Assessments should do two things. First, they should tell you what information your students know and what they don't know. Second, they should help reinforce what students already know while at the same time re-teaching any information students may not have learned the first time around. Tests, quizzes and worksheets don't necessarily do that. Those things tell you what you got right, what you got wrong and you are assigned a score to indicate a passing or failing grade. Learning doesn't necessarily involve grading and neither does assessing the knowledge of your students.

Learning is suppose to be fun... let me repeat that, learning is suppose to be fun, in addition to informative, enlightening and challenging. So too should assessing your students. I remember a number of evaluations where I specifically lost points because I did not assess my students at the end of the lesson. I told my principal that I hadn't built one into my lesson plan. I didn't do so primarily because I thought that by assessment what was meant was either a quiz or a test and if my evaluation didn't fall on a day when I quizzed a group, then I wouldn't have an assessment. I was told by an administrator, later, that I should always have an assessment... at least when I am being evaluated. I am passing on that same advice. When I teach, I teach for the week, meaning that there is one big lesson with mini lessons built in that will continue for the week. I may not assess until the end of the week or the beginning of the next week. If you are like me, you may or may not have an assessment scheduled for the end of each class, but you should make sure that you do have an assessment prepared for the end of your class when you are being formally evaluated. If an informal evaluation takes place and you fail to assess in your class, it will not be held against you – or at least it isn't suppose to be.

One thing that teachers do in the way of assessing their students is to give exit slips to their students at the end of every class. I am not huge fan of these, but if you need something quick and efficient, I suppose such a tactic will do. I advocate that in times when you need to assess students, which should be at the very least once a week, you should use tactics that do not create unnecessary anxiety amongst your students or do not come off as more of necessary evil and not a worthwhile venture that has a solid purpose. It was a struggle at times for me to figure out what a good assessment was; what worked with my students verses what didn't work, what information was I trying to see that my students knew, and if they were able to apply the information they learned in a practical way. That led me to the point where all roads meet discussed in this text; the place where cultural relevance, integrating technology, understanding my students, critical thinking, and collaboration came together. That place is what I affectionately refer to as assessology. By looking at the term you would reasonably believe that assessology means the study of assessing or assessment. My creating the word simple refers to a culturally relevant and engaging means to assessing student knowledge while integrating technology, popular culture, teamwork and a bit of pressure. Over my time, I have created a few ways of assessing my students. These tactics have been tested with good success. There have been some ideas that fell flat on their face. Those won't be discussed here. What I will share however are some of the methods behind the madness that I have successfully created and implemented over the years. Some of these means of assessing are things that you may have heard of and have even tried yourselves, others maybe a bit out of the ordinary. If you try them, you'll find out how practical and entertaining these can be.

Before I go into them, I would like to tell you what is involved on a fundamental level. The purpose of assessing as was already expressed is to learn of what your students know and impress upon them what they aren't necessarily sure of. The primary way of achieving this end is by questioning them. It is very important that you have a firm handle on exactly what you will be questioning your students about and how you intend on questioning them. These things largely depend upon the information you are looking to extract from their brains. You can ask a student about a fact and that only proves that they may or may not know that fact. You can also ask a student if they have a different way of going about solving a problem that someone has unsuccessfully attempted to solve, and their answer can tell you that they know facts and how to apply those facts to solve a problem, reflect on a situation and/or analyze the approach of others who previously attempted to address it. One of the best frameworks to follow with regards to the level of questioning you can deploy is *Bloom's Taxonomy of Questioning and Assessment*. Without getting too involved in explaining it, according to this framework, there are 6 levels of questioning:

1. Remembering, *recalling data or information*;
2. Understanding, *stating a problem in one's own words*;
3. Application, *applies what was learned in the classroom into novel situations anywhere*;

4. Analysis, *separates concepts into components so that its organizational structure is understood*
5. Evaluation, *make judgments about the value of ideas or materials*
6. Creation, *builds a structure or pattern from divers elements*

For more information on *Bloom's Taxonomy*, there are various online resources where you can get more knowledge on what this looks like with respect to the sort of questions asked in each level. My go to website for clarity on the questioning levels is http://www.nwlink.com/~donclark/hrd/bloom.html. There you will find all kinds of helpful information that you can apply to your classroom questioning.

When it comes to all of my assessology exercises, they each possess the following components: each exercise has each level of Bloom's built in, each exercise has extra credit points attached to them and all of my students have to participate, whether or not they want to. Even if a student starts out like they have no interest in participating, when they see the fun in participating you will win them over and they will join. If they choose not to join, your class will, 9 times out of 10, apply positive peer pressure to coerce them to join the group collectively. As I stated previously, these exercises are a culturally relevant and engaging means of assessing student knowledge while integrating technology, popular culture, teamwork and some pressure. At the end of the classes, my students walk out having engaged in an awesome experience designed to educate them and promote further study and application of what they've learned. While I have a number of trusty exercises in my stable, here are my starting five assessology drills:

1. <u>Jeopardy</u> – Jeopardy is an oldie but a goody and nonetheless effective. My students always love playing jeopardy and it is a great way to divide the class into teams to compete for points on their tests or quizzes. I usually play jeopardy with my students at the end of each unit prior to a major test. Thanks to this website <u>http://www.superteachertools.com/jeopardy/</u>, I am able to make as many games as humanly possible. Check out the website and play jeopardy with your students if you have yet to do so. This may be tough to do during an evaluation from an administrator, but this is a good exercise when prepping for a major test or exam.

2. <u>The Pyramid Game</u> – many years ago, Dick Clark hosted a show called the $10,000 Pyramid. Later, it became the $25,000 Pyramid and then came the $100,000 Pyramid. After all that money, they shifted the game to Celebrity Pyramid and contestants played to win money for charities. The point of the game was a team of two people were involved in a guessing game;

one person was given a noun that they had to describe to their partner without saying what it was while their partner guessed it. Teams had 1 minute to guess up to 7 items from a categorical list i.e. things found in a house or sports played outdoors. All you have to do to make this game applicable for your classroom is to create your own categorical lists based on a specified lesson or unit of study in your content area. You can have students make their guesses with only 1 minute, but I always give my students 2 minutes. This is a hit with the students and it is a great way to assess quickly when you only have a period to teach and assess. This is always great when evaluators are in the room.

3. <u>The Socratic Method</u> – this exercise puts the fear of God into my students. Some people would argue with me that making students fear doesn't teach them. I would argue that educators use fear tactics on a regular basis to achieve their desired goals of eliciting good behavior and high academic performance from students. In the spirit of Dr. Lore, I allow my students to have their notes and textbooks out to help them and I randomly choose them to answer questions. I start with a level 1 or level 2 Bloom's question and I work my way up the levels as I see fit. I never let a student get away with not providing me with an educated answer, I stare at them dead in the face and I wait for

an answer. The remainder of the class is to remain quiet and if I catch anyone speaking, they will be next to answer questions. Backing up that threat a few times keeps the classroom quiet, where the only sound you hear are those of pages turning. Those pages turning show me that my students are involved. Sure, they don't want to get a question wrong for fear of me constantly hovering over them but what is wrong with that? Some students relish the opportunity to go one-on-one with me to prove to me and their classmates that they know the material. That is an awesome thing. At the end of the class, I make sure to remind them that in college and specifically in law school (for all my future lawyers) that this is what they have to look forward to and so they ought to get use to it. This is also a good assessment exercise if you have a lesson that takes up half of your period; this can take up the other half.

4. Mr. Drill Sergeant – this exercise involves me, a whistle and me acting like I am an army sergeant. Now, I cannot yell at my students, but their punishments for getting answers wrong require their physical involvement. I either allow students to work in pairs or I make them work independently. The object here is simple. I go around the room, get in their face and ask them a question (I make sure to have plenty of mints that day). If they get a question wrong,

the penalty involves some sort of physical activity and repeating the answer over and over or a physical activity and an explanation of a better rational for an answer they've given. I have students drop and give me 20 push-ups or give me 25 jumping jacks or jog in place for 1 minute as they give me the answer that I am looking to hear. The students cannot stop laughing because when I am in character, I get quite animated, but they are penalized for laughing a little too much. My students get into this activity and the beauty of this exercise is that when the students get a bit out of hand, you can bring them right back because you can switch the funny to the serious really quickly; you can turn into a real life drill sergeant in the classroom when need be. This maybe an assessment you may want to save for a day you are not being evaluated because it can become a bit much in your room. But if you have good classroom management skills, you can knock it out of the park with this exercise; one day, I'll surprise my students with fatigues, a hat and army boots.

5. <u>Karaoke Day</u> – This is probably my absolute favorite of all the exercises. I order the students to write down 3 questions each about what we learned and write down 3 of their favorite songs. I collect the questions and the songs. I then split the class into teams of 2. I take the questions that everyone wrote and I ask both

teammates a question where they must look at their partner in the eyes as they both think about the answer and answer the question. If either of them laugh or get their question wrong, there is a penalty that they will both have to pay. If both students get their questions correct, they are spared and they receive 2 points on their next test or quiz. The penalty for incorrect answers or laughing prior to answering a question is they will have to either sing the correct answer or sing the phrase, *"I will not laugh when answering a question"* to the instrumental of one of the written songs amongst the student selections that I will randomly choose. All students are to participate and they have a ball... in most cases because hardly any of them can sing. There is so much fun had during this assessment that it ought to be illegal. But the potential for embarrassment involved with having to sing in front of their peers motivates many students to think and give correct answers when questioned. Are there students with public speaking and singing anxieties, sure there are, but I make sure that when those students have to perform, that I join them in the front of the room and sound so crazy that the attention is on me and not on them.

With all of these exercises, there is a lot of risk involved. There are some things that I described here that you believe that you cannot do with your students or that you know your students will object to doing; that may be true. But these exercises go back to chapter 1: knowing your team. Before you try anything new or tricky, make an educated guess as to how your population of students will respond. If you think the response will be positive, go for it. If not, wait until you feel more comfortable to do something like these exercises. Also, in order for you to get away with getting participation from your students when you wouldn't otherwise receive it, you must have a good relationship with your students; it comes with time. Rome wasn't built in a day and neither are good and strong relationships between students and teachers. Nevertheless, as your relationships grow stronger, so will the trust your students have in you to push them further and have a little bit of fun in the process.

STRATEGIES TO IMPLEMENT:

- Assessology refers to a culturally relevant and engaging means to assessing student knowledge while integrating technology, popular culture and collaboration.
- When creating assessments for your students, ensure that they are culturally relevant and engaging, integrating technology, popular culture, a little

pressure and current events to gain the ultimate objective – assessing student knowledge of the content.
- Be sure to include different levels of questioning within your assessments to ascertain not only the fact based knowledge your students gained during the lesson you taught, but also to ascertain their ability to take that knowledge and understand it, analyze it, evaluate it and use it to innovate.
- Make an educated guess as to the level to push your students with the consequences and rewards you associate with your assessments – knowing your team is essential to knowing what you can and cannot do.
- Use your judgment as to which assessments to use when being formally evaluated.
- ALWAYS have an assessment exercise prepared when being formally evaluated.

THE CLOSE

"Do not train a child to learn by force or harshness; but direct them to it by what amuses their minds, so that you may be better able to discover with accuracy the peculiar bent of the genius of each."

- Plato

One of the most important people in any sport, on any team, is the closer. The closer is the person who will close the game out for you; "seal the deal" if you will... they make sure that the victory is never in doubt. The greatest closer in my lifetime, in any sport was Michael Jordan, only the greatest basketball player ever and one of the greatest athletes of the 20th century. These days, Kobe Bryant, Tom Brady, and Tiger Woods (not so much lately) are the best closers in sports. In baseball, they have a pitcher who specializes in closing out games – he's the closer. The closer is often times paid more than starting pitchers. The closer is very important. The most important position in all of sports is quite possibly the NFL quarterback, and even he must be a great closer. Closing is indeed important to any aspect of our assignments in life. My father always taught me to always finish what I start. And with all of that being said, I want to close out this text with one more issue for you to ponder...

When it comes to Black and Hispanic/Latino kids in inner-city schools, educators need to ask themselves an honest question: do you care more about academic performance of students or student behavior? It seems to me that some educators tend to stress the latter a bit more than the former. I have a serious problem with this. Not because I don't think Black and Hispanic/Latino students, or any student for that matter, should be allowed or encouraged to be unruly, but my issue lies in the fact that some educators grocery shop when it comes to what they want to see in schools that are in high-poverty areas.

What is interesting to me is that teachers, school & district administrators as well as policy makers are very careful to not get into the business of raising Black and Hispanic/Latino students with high needs, yet these same people make it a point to stress that these very kids are to behave properly at all times. If a kid comes to school tired due to a lack of sleep because of a domestic issue and he or she sleeps in class and subsequently gets into it with their teacher, it is immediately a disciple issue. If a child comes to school and is constantly moving, cannot focus and is always talking, he or she is probably a candidate for medication to address attention deficit disorder or attention deficit hyperactivity disorder. If a student gets out of line, he or she is immediately referred to academic discipline. This happens to Blacks and Hispanic/Latinos across socio-economic lines, but in the high-poverty school, these matters are certainly concentrated: law and order trumps academic achievement and it is believed that if students are orderly, then they can learn. I would argue that if students are actually learning, then they will behave.

If you don't think that law and order take priority over academic achievement, maybe you should visit our nation's schools, specifically in high-poverty areas: many of these schools function like correctional facilities with their high security systems to keep students from getting out, buzzers to allow people in, metal detectors for students and visitors to keep weapons out and school security staff (who functions as a correctional staff). Not surprisingly, if we consider schools across the nation, the most frequently targeted for punishment in school often look—in terms of race, gender and socioeconomic status—a lot like smaller versions of the adults who are most likely to be targeted for incarceration in society (Singer, 1996). At the end of the day, students in these schools are simply contained; never expected to amount to anything more than people who live off the system either on public assistance or in prison.

In most schools and districts across the country, an examination of which students are most likely to be suspended, expelled, or removed from the classroom for punishment reveals that minorities (especially Blacks and Hispanics/Latinos), males and low achievers generally, are vastly over represented (Noguera, 2003). A 2012 U.S. Department of Education's Office of Civil Rights report reveals a number of unacceptable truths about Blacks and Hispanics/Latinos in our nation's schools:

- African Americans are over represented in the categories of students who receive in-school suspensions, out of school suspensions and expulsions when compared to Hispanics/Latinos and Whites.
- 70% of students involved in school related arrest or referred to law enforcement were African Americans and Hispanics/Latinos.
- Across all districts, African American students are 3½ times more likely to be suspended or expelled than their White peers
- In districts that reported expulsions under zero tolerance, Hispanic/Latino and African American students represents 45% of the student body, but 56% of the students expelled under such policies.

There is a pipeline from school to prison and many Black and Hispanic/Latino students in inner-city schools are funneled through it. Some will argue that there are schools where this is not the norm; schools where Black and Hispanic/Latino inner-city students do succeed, where academic performance is the focus of the school, and yes there are schools that are like this. However, if you control for student behavior, as many magnets and some charters schools do, of course you can have success. Schools that don't have a selection process; schools that teach with no respect of persons don't have the luxury of immediate academic success... they have the burden of establishing order. Policymakers as well as bureaucrats and lobbyists have facilitated this culture of law and order within inner-city schools... the mantra in many inner-city districts is that if you follow the rules, then you will be given the opportunity to learn. Zero tolerance policies are designed to ensure order. If a school has a uniform policy and a child comes to school out of uniform, he or she is often times sent home and will not be allowed to come back to school without being in full uniform. If a child is dismissed from the classroom for discipline reasons, he or she is referred to the in school suspension office for the remainder of that class period and in some cases for the rest of the day. Available evidence suggests that the adoption of zero tolerance policies related to discipline and order by school districts across the United States has contributed to a significant increase in the number of children who are being suspended and expelled from school (Sikba, 2000). Let's be honest with ourselves; when it comes to teaching Blacks and Hispanic/Latinos in inner-city schools, the hope and desire is to teach them how to be functional law abiding citizens so that they don't become criminals because quite frankly, agenda driven media continuously perpetuates the belief that people of color are prone to criminality and are incapable living within the structure of American society.

Zero tolerance policies encourage students, not to get focused, but rather get unfocused. Suspensions of any kind reduce a student's time in the classroom, facilitating their failure in their coursework and on the high stakes testing that unfortunately guard their promotion, graduation and entry into college. Schools that suspend large numbers of students, or that suspend small numbers of students frequently, typically find themselves so preoccupied with discipline and control that they have little time to address the conditions that influences teaching and learning (Noguera, 2003). In a 2006 study conducted by the Bill and Melinda Gates Foundation, 32% of high school dropouts quit school because they had missed too much classroom instruction and couldn't "catch up," while 66% of students claimed they dropped out because they weren't motivated to work hard, yet they also claimed they would have worked harder if more had been expected of them (Lara, 2013).

For the teacher, administrator and non-educator taxpayer, racism has little to do with perception; fear and ignorance plays a bigger role. For the individuals who are the agenda setters and policymakers via lobbying dollars in the form of campaign funding, backroom deals and media blitzes, fear and ignorance has little to do with the basis of their activity; maintaining the social order does. Education is big business and to maintain the failing atmosphere of inner-city schools where law and order takes precedent, business is even bigger. Everyone else is benefitting from the current state of urban schooling except the students; the people who are suppose to be benefitting from schooling in the first place.

    The connotation of being a "good" student has changed from having good grades to having good behavior and conduct. Teachers and administrators tend to want to help the "good" students more than the disruptive students; whether or not the disruptive students are actually intelligent doesn't matter. The disruptive behavior of even the most intelligent of students often disqualifies him or her from receiving the attention they need to maximize their potential as students and citizens. The way many inner-city schools function do nothing but "teach" Black and Hispanic/Latino students how to follow rules, memorize and repeat to pass standardized tests and not to kill each other until after graduation when they are no longer the responsibility of the school. It is not in the design that most students in these schools become socially mobile... poverty is concentrated in urban areas and inner-cities... poor education systems are as well. In fact, the only socially mobile people are some of the people who come to work each day from the suburbs. Good students from these schools may or may not know enough to achieve gainful employment so they can create a good life for themselves. But good students from these schools do know how to stand in line at public places to wait their turn, good students from these schools do know not to challenge those in authority under any circumstances; good students from these schools know their place. The million dollar question for all "stakeholders" to answer is if they want Black and Hispanic/Latino inner-city students to determine their course in society or to know their place in society. What is your answer?

Please ensure that in your classroom, the good students are the ones who study hard, engage in classroom activities, are critical thinkers and make their peers better students and their communities' better places in addition to being well behaved. The strategies in this book will help you cultivate good students within your classroom. The strategies in this book will help with your classroom management. Implement this offensive game plan ASAP. In urban education, we (educators) are always on the defense... but remember that one of the keys to having a good defense is having a good offense.

Giving Thanks

Any time you intend on taking on an endeavor such as writing a book, it takes a lot of support to make it happen. As the parent of a toddler, I owe a debt of gratitude, as well as a candle light dinner, to my lovely wife. She continues to be my biggest cheerleader and most staunch critic. I love her with all of my heart and I appreciate her for her honesty, understanding nature and tolerance of my work ethic.

I would also like to thank the LEAP Academy community. I want to thank many of my co-laborers in this vocation. I would like to personally thank Mr. Brian Kam for his wonderful presentation on new technologies for the classroom. Because of his excellent research, I was able to provide it as a resource in this book. I also want to thank many of the administrators who have supported me along the way especially Nancy Ruiz and Barbara Dunlap. I would also like to particularly thank Dr. Nestor Collazo, a man who has taught me much about how to go about the business of teaching.

I would like to thank my students. Without my students, I would not be teacher or professional that I am today. I have learned so much from the many students that I have crossed paths with over the years. The love I have for my students is never ending. The LEAP Academy University

Charter School Class of 2013 and the LEAP Academy STEM Class of 2014 hold a special place in my heart. These are the classes that have had the greatest impact on me both professionally and personally. I pray that each one of you is guided by the almighty in reaching you potential to making this world a better place; shout out to Destiny Bingham for writing me such a touching letter at the end of her sophomore year, to Sierra Sanabria for drawing that crazy picture of me, and shout out to the students who participated in my survey used for this book. To the countless names of students whom I did not mention, you are not forgotten or without my gratitude, appreciation and love.

I would like to thank my colleague, my co-laborer in this ministry in educating children of color, my friend and trusted ally Mr. Khary Golden. Through our work, we have forged a bond that has extended outside our school walls. Your camaraderie in this mission; your wisdom and your insight have helped me be a better educator and a better man. Our district is indeed a better place because of your leadership and passion for this work.

While writing this book, I was in the process of physically losing my grandmother. She was in the hospital during the entire month of January of 2013 while I was continuing to write this book. We lost her on February 3rd. I took time off from the book and everything to devote to handling any and all business with relation to her passing.

My grandmother was indeed my rock. She was my biggest cheerleader, she has always been there for me and she was the person who led me to Jesus Christ. I love her dearly. Never have I lost someone so close to me. Her departure has been tough. But I thank God that she is in that great city where there is no more crying and no more pain.

Lastly, I want to give reverence to my Lord and savior Jesus Christ. Without Him in my life, I can do nothing. I thank Him for His patience, His grace, His mercy and His love. I am appreciative of the gifts He has bestowed upon me and I pray that I am able to use them to build His kingdom, to benefit all people to increase the number of His people.

APPENDICES
THE PLAYBOOK

Table of Contents

Appendix 1 - p155
Student Survey Template (Chapter 2)

Appendix 2 - p156
Case Study #1: Cultural Differences - *World Cultures* (Chapter 6)

Appendix 3 - p158
Case Study #2: Prohibition - *U.S. History* (Chapter 6)

Appendix 4 - p160
Debating Profile Assessment (Chapter 7)

Appendix 5 - p162
Debating Pre/Post Assessment (Chapter 7)

Appendix 6 - p164
Debate Judging Form (Chapter 7)

Appendix 7 - p165
Creating Memes (Chapter 8)

Appendix 8 - p167
Twittersations (Chapter 8)

Appendix 9 - p170
New Technologies for Your Class (Chapter 8)

Appendix 10 - p174
Reference List

APPENDIX 1 – STUDENT SURVEY TEMPLATE

*Taken from chapter 2

Directions: Answer each question honestly and truthfully. Make a check in the box that applies.

Gender   _____
Race/Ethnicity   _____
Grade Level   _____
GPA   _____
Age   _____

	Always	Frequent	Occasional	Rarely	Never
Your teachers motivate and/or inspire you to work hard in school					
Your parents or guardians motivate and/or inspire you to work hard in school					
You are disciplined and/or punished for your behavior in school					

	Yes	No	Not Sure
My teachers cared about my success as a student			
My teachers cared about me as an individual			
My teachers could identify with and understand me			

APPENDIX 2 – CASE STUDY #1: CULTURAL DIFFERENCES

*Taken from chapter 6

Background

Jose is a young man who lives in Camden, New Jersey. Although Jose was born in Puerto Rico, he was raised in the U.S. since the age of 3 years old. Although he understands the Spanish language, he cannot speak it. He parents retain many traditions and customs of Puerto Rican culture, while Jose does not.

Scenario

Jose is attending the sweet 16 ceremony and party of his girlfriend Amanda. Amanda was born and raised in Puerto Rico and she recently moved from the island 2 years ago. She is fluent in both Spanish and English and retains much of her culture. Amanda's parents deeply value their Puerto Rican heritage and are concerned that the integrity of the sweet 16 ceremony will be compromised if Jose is allowed to participate as Amanda's boyfriend. Jose listens to rap music, he is unaware of traditional Puerto Rican dances and Amanda's parents have a problem with the fact that Jose cannot speak Spanish. Amanda's parents have asked her to replace Jose with someone else more "familiar" with the culture.

Activity

Amanda has come to you, her friend, to seek advice for what to say to her parents. She does not want to replace Jose but she is unsure of what she should say and the various reasons for keeping Jose. Please give her some advice, based on what you've learned about culture so far. Write a 1 paragraph essay containing the following elements:

- Introductory sentence
- Thesis
- Counter Argument
- 3 Supporting Points
- Conclusion

APPENDIX 3 – CASE STUDY #2: PROHIBITION

*Taken from chapter 6

Background

Mr. Malcolm is a very well known owner of a beer factory. This factory has been in his family for years. The family business started in his native Jamaica. When Mr. Malcolm's father moved here in the 1970's, he built a factory in Philadelphia. Mr. Malcolm took over the business just 10 years ago. He has built more factories in New York City and in Washington D.C. His cousin, Zaire Malcolm, was jealous that he was never in charge of the family business. He turned to selling illegal narcotics instead. For the last 10 years, Zaire has built a drug empire from Jamaica that spans the entire East Coast of the United States. Mr. Malcolm has asked his cousin to stop but Zaire has refused.

Scenario

Last year, a local Congresswoman from NJ's 1st District, Ms. Brittany Ruiz, lost her daughter to alcoholic poisoning. Her daughter, Myesha, died from having too many beers at a college party at her school, Temple University. According to the police report, she drank over thirty 20-oz bottles of Mr. Malcolm's premium brew. A few months later, Congresswoman Ruiz introduced a new prohibition law to be passed nationally—she called it *Myesha's Law* in honor of her daughter who passed away. When Mr. Malcolm heard of the news, he was sad for the Congresswoman's loss, but he did not believe she should hinder his business, nor would passing such a law prevent more death from drinking. Mr. Malcolm wrote in a letter to the Congresswoman that he was sorry for her loss, but to consider passing tough anti-drug laws. Mr. Malcolm was requested by Congress to testify on behalf of the Liquor Lobbyists. Mr. Malcolm agreed to go and as he was in the train on the way, he considered ratting out his cousin out to prevent a ban on alcoholic beverages in the U.S.

Activity

Should Mr. Malcolm rat out his cousin in an effort to prevent a national ban on alcoholic substances? What exactly should Mr. Malcolm say to prevent a ban on alcoholic substances? Write a 1 paragraph essay containing the following elements:

- Introductory sentence
- Thesis
- Counter Argument
- 3 Supporting Points
- Conclusion Sentence

APPENDIX 4 – DEBATING PROFILE ASSESSMENT

*Taken from chapter 7

Directions: These questions will be used to assess skills as pre-debaters and to generate teams.

	SPEAKER	RESEARCHER	ORGANIZER
Of the following choices, where are you are most likely to shop	*Tele Communications Store*	*Bookstore*	*Office Supply Store*
Of the choices given, which career are you most likely to choose	*Talk Show Host*	*Librarian*	*Event Planner*
The interest should be used for which of the following	*Communication*	*Information*	*Organizing Events*
Of the following choices, what would you enjoy doing the most	*Talking With Friends*	*Learning New Things*	*Planning Events*
The most important thing about talking to people	*Actually Talking To Them*	*Learning About How to Speak to Them*	*Gathering Your Thoughts*
As a student, the most important thing to do is	*Ask Questions*	*Study*	*Get Organized*
A great public speaker is someone who	*Speaks Clearly*	*Understands What They Are Talking About*	*Present Information Clearly*
Of the following choices, what would you rather do	*Talk About Music*	*Read About Music*	*Organize Your Own Music*
Of the following choices, what would you rather watch	*A Play*	*A Documentary*	*A Pet Competition*

Of the following choices, what is the best television show	*Dr. Phil*	*E-True Hollywood Story*	*Extreme Home Makeover*
TOTAL POINTS			
	Speaker Points	Researcher Points	Organizer Points

APPENDIX 5 – DEBATING PRE/POST ASSESSMENT

*Taken from chapter 7

Directions: Rate your ability in doing the following from 1 (Very Weak) to 5 (Very Strong). Please answer each question as best as you can.

	Very Weak -1	Weak - 2	Fair -3	Strong -4	Very Strong - 5
Your ability to debate others formally					
Your ability to see both sides of an argument					
Your ability to work on teams					
Your ability to write in an organized manner					
Your ability to think critically					

Level of self-confidence to writing, researching and public speaking					
Level of knowledge of current events					

APPENDIX 6 – DEBATE JUDGING FORM

*Taken from chapter 7

Directions: This outline is to help you judge the teams on debating days. Students are to answer the following questions to the best of your abilities..

Topic: _____

Team 1: _____

Team 2: _____

1. What is the history surrounding the topic. What is the problem?

2. What is the exact problem?

3. Which group do you agree with and why?

4. Provide 3 supporting points in favor for the debate topic

5. Provide 3 supporting points against the debate topic

Final Vote: _____

Explain Why:

APPENDIX 7 – CREATING MEMES

*Taken from chapter 8

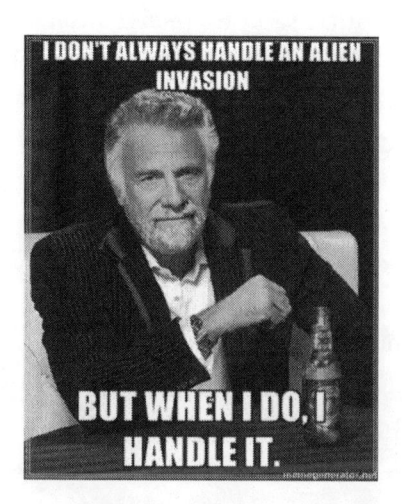

According to Webster's Dictionary, a meme is an idea, behavior, style, or usage that spreads from person to person within a culture, which can change over time. An internet meme is the same, however it spreads throughout the world wide web. An internet meme can take any kind of form i.e. an image, video, picture, website or hashtag, and it can use correct or incorrect grammar and/or spelling. Internet meme's are often used to promote various truths, expose various errors, provide commentary, provide parody/comedy and market information. Your students are familiar with memes and some student have created their own in their spare time; whether or not their creations were productive ones is another discussion. However, you can assign such a task where students create their own for your classroom and productive ones at that.

Whatever your respective content area is, you can create an assignment where students can create their own memes in class or at home. Students can work in groups or

165

independently. Depending on the technology at your disposal, you can be very basic and use the art/paint program on your pc or laptop or you can go as far and use programs like Adobe Photoshop. When putting your assignment together, you can install a number of rules that fit what it is you are trying to do in your classroom. It goes without saying that any foul, prejudicial or discriminatory language, expressions, images or phrases are allowed in any student created meme. So long as students follow that rule of respect and whatever other rules you set in your specified assignment, this should be a fun experience for the students. Once finished, you can allow students the opportunity to present them to the class for a presentation grade. Another suggestion would be to allow your students to vote on the best meme created and provide the winning student or students with a prize.

In my class on world history, I used this assignment on our unit about Africa. I asked my students to create a meme that has to do with traditional village rituals; rituals that are celebrated throughout the world or rituals that are viewed as human rights violations throughout the world. I had a set of rules and here is one of the creations I received:

APPENDIX 8 - TWITTERSATIONS

*Taken from chapter 8

One of the great inventions of communication to land on planet earth was the internet. The internet allows us the opportunity to community with each other in ways we never before thought were possible. One such avenue for communicating with friends and strangers alike is Twitter. Who knew that we could go even further than just emailing and simple chatting; Twitter allows us to send information and converse with multiple people rapidly. Twitter is an online social network that allows users to read and send text-like messages called tweets. These tweets help keep long-winded individuals short-winded with its allowance of only 140 characters.

One of the cool things about Twitter is that you can converse with famous people. Sure, you can follow celebrities and see what they are doing but the fun comes when I am able to speak to someone famous because of something that they said that happened to peak my interest. I have had a number of conversations with people. During the February of this year, I commented on a tweet from Erykah Badu. She was performing in Philadelphia and I made a comment in excitement about her performing that night. In 5 minutes I got a retweet – a retweet is when someone retweets something that you tweeted. All of her followers then saw my tweet and I got new followers who now read my tweets (followers automatically receive any tweets that you send). I also had an encounter of the negative kind with the host of the ESPN show *Around the Horn*, Tony Reali... I made a statement regarding my thoughts on the racial composition of the guest and it relating to who wins and who loses. It turned into a very ugly argument. Quite honestly, I was shocked he kept going back and forth. Nevertheless, I have the transcripts from that conversation and the retweet from Ms. Badu. Like I said, Twitter lets you do something "regular" people would otherwise not be able to do with celebrities; give them a piece of your mind.

In the case of your classroom, you can craft an assignment where your students speak, or attempt to speak, with a celebrity or athlete. The best way to facilitate a conversation with a famous person is to ask them a question or specifically find their views on a specific subject. You can create the question/topic for your students to ask the famous person of their choice. With respect to grading criteria, you can give grades according to the length of your conversation, which famous person(s) you spoke with, or both. You can also use this as a friendly competition amongst the students in your classes.

Here are some basics you can use as rules to help you when crafting your assignments for your class:

1. You must cut and past the actual twitter conversation from the site (you and the celebrity) on a word document when submitting the assignment
2. You must hashtag all your questions / comments with the following: (You specify the term/phrase ex. #RM312His). Without it, submissions will be disqualified. Remember to keep hashtag term/phrase short. Due to the 140 character limit, you students will need as much space as possible to converse with the famous person.

3. Twitter conversations should not take place during school time. Any conversation submitted during school hours will be disqualified (Use your discretion with respect to study hall time or lunch time used by student to communicate on Twitter).
4. Any vulgar, foul or discriminatory language said by the student within any tweet will lead to the disqualification of said student submission.

APPENDIX 9 – NEW TECHNOLOGIES FOR YOUR CLASS

*Taken from chapter 8

The following are web resources, with addresses and descriptions, which can help with furthering the instruction within your classroom outside of the classroom. All descriptions are taken from the website of each resource tool.

Medium:	Show Me
Purpose:	Podcasting/recording
Device:	ipad
Description:	ShowMe is a global learning community - a place where anyone can learn or teach anything. The ShowMe iPad app lets you create lessons using a whiteboard. The app is free and there is no limit what you can teach! Our community has created millions of ShowMes, from chemistry to history to football strategy - and more knowledge is being shared every day.
Cost:	Free
Address:	www.showme.com

Medium:	Explain Everything
Purpose:	Podcasting/recording
Device:	ipad
Description:	Explain Everything is an easy-to-use design tool that lets you annotate, animate, and narrate explanations and presentations. You can create dynamic interactive lessons, activities, assessments, and tutorials using Explain Everything's flexible and integrated design. Use Explain Everything as an interactive whiteboard using the iPad2 video display.
Cost:	$2.99
Address:	www.explaineverything.com

Medium: Educreations
Purpose: Podcasting/recording
Device: ipad
Description: Educreations is a global community where anyone can teach what they know and learn what they don't. We're on a mission to democratize learning by extending the reach of great teaching.
Cost: Free
Address: www.educreations.com

Medium: Jing
Purpose: Podcasting/recording
Device: Desktop/laptop
Description: Jing gives you the basic tools to start sharing images and short videos of your computer screen. Capture an image of what you see on your computer screen with Jing. Simply select any window or region that you want to capture, mark up your screenshot with a text box, arrow, highlight or picture caption, and decide how you want to share it. Select any window or region that you would like to record, and Jing will capture everything that happens in that area.
Cost: Free
Address: http://www.techsmith.com/jing.html

Medium: SyncPad
Purpose: Interactive whiteboard & podcasting/recording
Device: ipad & web browsers
Description: Make your classes truly interactive and fun with SyncPad. Many schools are already using SyncPad as a key application in their 1-to-1 iPad programs. Imagine bringing the whiteboard or class presentation right to the students' desks in the classroom or at home. Use SyncPad to interact directly with your students. Let them answer your questions on the whiteboard from their seats.

Cost: Free
Address: https://syncpadapp.com/

Medium: Doceri
Purpose: Interactive whiteboard
Device: ipad & desktop/laptop
Description: Doceri is the professional iPad interactive whiteboard and screencast recorder with sophisticated tools for hand-drawn graphics and built-in remote desktop control. Originally designed for teachers, Doceri is used by creative individuals in myriad roles and professions from education to entertainment.Create hand-drawn lessons, presentations and graphics and share them as still images, PDFs or audio/video screencasts - or mirror anything you've created to Apple TV via AirPlay.
Cost: $30 License
Address: www.doceri.com

Medium: Keepvid
Purpose: Recording YouTube video
Device: Desktop/laptop & tablet
Description: Download any streaming videos for your own PC or laptop storage
Cost: Free
Address: keepvid.com

Medium: Listen to YouTube
Purpose: Download
Device: Desktop/laptop & tablet
Description: ListenToYouTube.com is the most convenient online application for converting YouTube flash video to MP3 audio. This service is fast, free, and requires no signup. All you need is a YouTube URL, and our software will transfer the video to our server, extract the MP3, and give you a link to download the audio file.
Cost: Free
Address: http://www.listentoyoutube.com/index.php

Medium:	Live Binders
Purpose:	Course outlining/online course capable
Device:	Desktop/laptop & tablet
Description:	We created LiveBinders so that you could do with digital information what you do with the piles of papers on your desk - organize them into nice presentable containers - like 3-ring binders on your shelf. With our online binders you can combine all of your cloud documents, website links and upload your desktop documents - to then easily access, share, and update your binders from anywhere..
Cost:	Free
Address:	www.livebinders.com

Medium:	Class Dojo
Purpose:	Classroom Management Tool
Device:	Desktop/laptop & tablet
Description:	ClassDojo is a classroom tool that helps teachers improve behavior in their classrooms quickly and easily. It also captures and generates data on behavior that teachers can share with parents and administrators. Better learning behaviors, smoother lessons and hassle-free data - and its free!
Cost:	Free
Address:	www.classdojo.com

APPENDIX 10 - REFERENCE LIST

Advancement Project. (2010). *Test, Punish, and Push Out: How Zero Tolerance and High Stakes Testing Funnel Youth into the School-to-Prison Pipeline.* Washington D.C.: Advancement Project.

Civil Rights Data Collection. (2012). *Revealing New Truths About Our Nation's Schools.* Washington D.C.: United States Department of Education Office for Civil Rights.

Delpit, L., & White-Bradley, P. (2003). Educating or Imprisoning the Spirit: Lessons from Ancient Egypt. *Theory Into Practice* , 283-288.

Hamovitch, B. (1997). *Staying After School.* Westport: Praeger Publishers.

Howard, G. (2006). *We Can't Teach What We Don't Know.* New York: Teacher College Press.

Johnson, T., Boyden, J., & Pitts, W. (2001). *Racial Profiling and Punishment in the U.S. Public Schools: How Zero Tolerance Policies & High Stakes Testing Subvert Academic Excellence and Racial Equality.* 2001: Applied Research Center.

Lara, C. (2013, January 11). *Suspending to Mentorship: How to Curb the School-to-Prison Pipeline.* Retrieved January 11, 2013, from The Huffington Post: http://www.huffingtonpost.com/cristina-lara/suspending-to-mentorship-_b_2457842.html

MetLife. (2012). *The MetLife Survey of the American Teacher: Preparing Students for College and Careers.* New York: Metropolitian Life Insurance Company.

Metropolitan Life. (2001). *The American Teacher.* Washington D.C.: Metropolitan Life.

Miller, R. R. (2013). Choosing Discipleship Over the Veil. In C. Miller, R. R. (2012). *The Double D's of Destruction: How Our Distracted And Desensitized Consciousness Is Destroying Our*

Communities And Failing Our Children. Camden: ClarkMiller Publishing C/O CreateSpace Independent Publishing Platform.

National Geographic Education. (2013, March 6). *Urban Area.* Retrieved March 6, 2013, from National Geographic Education Beta: http://education.nationalgeographic.com/education/encyclopedia/urban-area/?ar_a=1

Newmann, F. (1992). *Student Engagement anc Achievement in American Secondary Schools.* New York: Teachers College Press.

Noguera, P. A. (2007). How Listening to Students Can Help Schools to Improve. *Theory Into Practice* , 205-211.

Noguera, P. A. (2003). Schools, Prisons, and Social Implications of Punishment: Rethinking Disciplinary Practices. *Theory Into Practice* , 341-350.

Ogbu, J. (1995). Cultural Problems in Minority Education: Their Interpretations and Consequences Part 1: Theoretical Background. *The Urban Review , 27* (3), 189-205.

Ogbu, J. (1995). Cultural Problems in Minority Education: Their Interpretations and Consequences Part 2: Case Studies. *The Urban Review , 27* (4), 271-297.

Schott Foundation for Public Education. (2010). *Yes We Can: The Schott 50 State Report on Public Education and Black Males.* Cambridge: Schott Foundation for Public Education.

Sikba, R. (2000). When Is Disproportionality Discrimination? The Overrepresentation of Black Students in School Suspension. In W. Ayers, B. Dorhn, & R. Ayers, *Zero Tolerance: Resisting the Drive For Punishment in Our Schools* (p. 23). New York: The New Press.

Singer, S. (1996). *Recriminalizing Delinquency.* Cambridge: Cambridge University Press.

Steinberg, L. (1996). *Beyond the Classroom: The Failure of School Reform.* New York: Simon and Schuster.

Thompson, G. L. (2007). *Up Where We Belong: Helping African American and Latino Students Rise In School and In Life.* San Francisco: Jossey Bass.

Thompson, G. L., & Allen, T. G. (2012). Four Effects of the High Stakes Testing Movement on African Americans K-12 Students. *The Journal of Negro Education* , 218-302.

Toldson, I. (2012, October 22). *How Race Matters In The Classroom.* Retrieved from The Root: http://www.theroot.com/views/how-race-matters-classroom?page=0,1

Weeks, J. R. (2010). Defining Urban Areas. In T. Rashad, & C. Jurgens, *Remote Sensing of Urban and Suburban Areas* (pp. 33-45). New York: Springer Science Business Media.

Weiner, L. (2003). Why Is Classroom Management So Vexing to Urban Teachers. *Theory Into Practice* , 305-312.

Weinstein, C., Curran, M., & Tomlinson-Clarke, S. (2003). Culturally Responsive Classroom Management: Awareness Into Action. *Theory Into Practice* , 269-276.

Wiggan, G. (2007). Race, School Achievement & Educational Inequality: Towards a Students-Based Inquiry Perspective. *Review of Educational Research* , 310-333.

Dear Mr. Miller,

Hi. How's my baby Jackson? Call me after he's potty-trained if you need a babysitter ☺ (I don't do diapers -_-).

Anyway, I'm writing this letter to thank you for the experience I've had with being taught by you this year.

All my other history teachers have failed terribly at teaching me anything worth remembering. Half of the reason I don't remember is my fault because I find history boring. But all your charades and games helped me reflect on everything we learned this year.

Also, you helped me find my "inner debater." I don't like disagreements or fighting, but sometimes they are necessary. In a way, you taught me how to be a stronger fighter.

It is for all these things that I appreciate your teachings and will remember your class. I hope I see you next year ☺.

Love, Destiny

P.S: I don't change the channel when the news reporter talks about polotics anymore. Aren't you proud of me? :D

Made in the USA
Lexington, KY
24 May 2013